OPPOSING HITLER
ADAM VON TROTT ZU SOLZ,
1909–1944

'To Strive and Not to Yield'

OPPOSING HITLER

ADAM VON TROTT ZU SOLZ,
1909–1944

KENNETH A. E. SEARS

sussex
ACADEMIC
PRESS
Brighton • Chicago • Toronto

Copyright © Kenneth A. E. Sears, 2009, 2011.

The right of Kenneth A. E. Sears to be identified as Author of this work has been asserted in accordance with the Copyright, Designs and Patents Act 1988.

2 4 6 8 10 9 7 5 3 1

First published in hardcover 2009, reprinted in paperback 2011 by
SUSSEX ACADEMIC PRESS
PO Box 139
Eastbourne BN24 9BP

Distributed in North America by
SUSSEX ACADEMIC PRESS
Independent Publishers Group
814 N. Franklin Street
Chicago, IL 60610

All rights reserved. Except for the quotation of short passages for the purposes of criticism and review, no part of this publication may be reproduced, stored in a retrieval system or transmitted in any form or by any means, electronic, mechanical, photocopying, recording or otherwise, without the prior permission of the publisher.

British Library Cataloguing in Publication Data
A CIP catalogue record for this book is available from the British Library.

Library of Congress Cataloging-in-Publication Data
Sears, Kenneth A. E.
 Opposing Hitler : Adam von Trott du Solz, 1909–1944 : "To strive and not to yield" / Kenneth A.E. Sears.
  p. cm.
 Includes bibliographical references and index.
 ISBN 978-1-84519-282-2 (hardcover : alk. paper)
 ISBN 978-1-84519-472-7 (pbk. : alk. paper)
  1. Trott zu Solz, Adam von, 1909–1944. 2. Anti-Nazi movement—Biography. 3. Anti-Nazi movement—Germany. 4. Hitler, Adolf, 1889–1945—Assassination attempt, 1944 (July 20) 5. Political activists—Germany—Biography. 6. Germany. Auswärtiges Amt—Officials and employees—Biography. 7. Germany—History—1933-1945. I. Title.
 DD256.3.T76S43 2010
 943.086092—dc22
 [B]   2009025781

Typeset and designed by Sussex Academic Press, Brighton & Eastbourne.

This book is printed on acid-free paper.

Contents

Preface and Acknowledgements   vii
Foreword by Diana Walford, Principal of Mansfield College   ix
Foreword by David Marquand, Former Principal of Mansfield College   xii
List of Illustrations   xv

1   Early Years   1

2   University Life – Munich and Göttingen   4

3   Mansfield College   7

4   University Life – Göttingen and Berlin   13

5   Rhodes Scholar   15

6   The Years 1933–1936   19

7   The Far East   21

8   Return to Germany and to Resistance   23

9   The 3rd of September 1939   31

10   The Plea for Recognition   34

11   The Kreisau Circle   39

12   Fanning the Flames of Resistance   42

13   The Year 1944   46

Contents

14	Final Preparations	59
15	The 20th of July 1944	64
16	Aftermath	68
17	The Allied Reaction	78
18	The Military Situation	83
19	Epilogue	85

Short Biographies   87
Notes   92
Bibliography   95
Index   97

Preface and Acknowledgements

On Thursday, 20 July 1944, the late evening BBC news bulletin carried reports of an attempt on Hitler's life. For the previous few weeks we had all been following keenly the progress of the Allied forces after the invasion of Normandy on 6 June. The news from Germany was seen as a step in heralding the end of the war. Within a few weeks it became clear that Hitler was determined to continue the unequal struggle, at whatever the cost, and the world moved into a sixth winter of fighting and heartbreak.

Twenty years later I was listening to a sermon being delivered in the chapel of Mansfield College, Oxford, by the Principal, Dr John Marsh, in which he referred to Adam von Trott zu Solz who had studied theology in the college in 1929 and who was one of the leaders of the resistance to Hitler in Nazi Germany. They were contemporaries as students and forged a strong friendship.

My interest in Adam von Trott was quickened and the brief entry in my schoolboy diary for 20 July – 'bomb attempt on Hitler' – began to be clothed with a richness which mere words cannot supply. The events of that day, and all that led to them, became real and active instead of being merely a historical record.

This account of his life and his struggle against Nazism is set within the context of the anti-Nazi resistance as it developed within Germany in the 1930s and 1940s. In attempting to glean, as far as it is possible after the passage of years, the atmosphere in Germany in the 1930s and during the war, I have been helped by German friends who have spoken of their lives in the Hitler Youth Movement and in the German army.

I acknowledge particularly the co-operation and help of some of those who knew him and have spoken of his friendship, especially the late John Marsh, Lawrence Wheeler and C. E. Dean. I am also grateful to Mrs Madeline Clayton, the daughter of Charles Collins of Balliol College, who sent me photographs and papers from her father's collection in connection with his friendship with Adam; the staff of the National Archives; the staff of the National Newspaper Library; the Librarian of Mansfield College, Alma Jenner; the former Warden of Rhodes House,

Preface and Acknowledgements

Oxford, Sir Anthony Kenny; the staff of the Kent County Library Service; and the many friends, far too numerous to mention, who have shown interest in my research and with whom I have spent many hours in conversation; and, most importantly, three successive Principals of Mansfield College, Dennis Trevelyan, Professor David Marquand and Dr Diana Walford for their encouragement.

My most sincere thanks go to Dr Clarita von Trott zu Solz who has encouraged and helped me in so many ways. When I started this work, she very kindly went through her family archives and sent me copies of his letters and other relevant papers. She and her family have been most kind in their hospitality on my visits to Germany and our many conversations have been of inestimable value.

Foreword by Diana Walford,
Principal of Mansfield College

I have known the author, Kenneth Sears, ever since I came to Mansfield College in 2002, as its tenth Principal. It was the College's second Principal, William Boothby Selbie, who, in 1929, was responsible for introducing Adam von Trott zu Solz to the College. This was also Adam's introduction to the seductive world of Oxford University, a world which was to play such an important role in his tragically foreshortened life. Although Adam studied at Mansfield for only one term in 1929, Selbie and he remained in contact for very many years.

Shortly after taking up my post in 2002, I heard about Adam von Trott's relationship to Mansfield and saw the pillar in the College chapel that bore an inscription in his memory and which had been unveiled, by his grandson, earlier that year. Only some time later did I find out that Kenneth had, for many years, been in the throes of writing a book about Adam's life. Eventually, after some urging, I was granted the privilege of reading it. I read the manuscript from cover to cover in one sitting (as I have just reread it in preparing this Foreword) and urged him to have it published. With great modesty he demurred and seemed set on continuing indefinitely with his research. It became a standing joke between us, on each occasion we met, that I would enquire whether he had yet embarked on finding a publisher, only to be met with a slightly sheepish denial. Finally, it was thanks to the efforts of a member of Mansfield's Senior Common Room, Professor Neville Brown, who took the initiative to introduce Kenneth to his own publisher, Sussex Academic Press, that the book was accepted for publication.

It is a remarkable book, which grips the attention like a novel but which, in truth, chronicles the real-life exploits of a man of huge courage, great nobility of spirit and a passionate desire to rid his beloved country of the scourge of Nazism. Much of the story is told via the medium of Adam's own words, either in letters he wrote or relayed by his family and friends. The author has enjoyed privileged access, through Adam's widow, Dr Clarita von Trott zu Solz, to the family archives. The inclusion of this material gives the book an immediacy and a poignancy that a mere retelling of the facts could not convey.

It is fair to say that Adam's single term at Mansfield was a formative time for him and was responsible for his determination to return to Oxford to continue his studies, as he did subsequently through his Rhodes Scholarship to study Philosophy, Politics and Economics at Balliol. It also marked the formation of the extensive network of friends and acquaintances in England that was to feature so prominently in his efforts to draw this country's attention, in the early 1930s, to the evils of the emerging National Socialist party and their criminally odious leader, Adolf Hitler.

It was a source of enormous frustration to Adam that his advice was at various times disbelieved, ignored or repudiated as unreliable. It would, one hopes, be of considerable gratification to him to know how thoroughly we now recognise the truth of his warnings and marvel at the extent to which he was prepared to sacrifice his own life in order to destroy the cancer in the midst of German society. Even after the unsuccessful coup on 20 July 1944, Adam is quoted as saying that he was pleased that the plot had taken place – it was a historical fact and that at least was something.

Adam continued to speak of Mansfield for many years after he had been here, just as almost eighty years on, we continue to speak of him. He was, as his close friend and confidante, Missie, said, "a man completely out of the ordinary" – and we salute his memory.

In 2004, to commemorate the 60th Anniversary of the plot to assassinate Hitler and Adam's role in it, Mansfield College hosted the first in a series of Adam von Trott Memorial Lectures, which was delivered by Professor Timothy Garton Ash and entitled 'Are there Moral Foundations of European Power?' Dr Keith Clements (2007) and Professor David Marquand (2008) have been the two subsequent Lecturers. Dr Clements' address took place at the German Embassy and was preceded by a most moving introduction by the Deputy German Ambassador, who spoke of the moral value of those who, like Adam, resisted the National Socialist dictatorship and were willing to give their lives for their beliefs and for their country.

At the inaugural Lecture, an appeal was launched to raise money to provide a scholarship for young German politics scholars to spend a term in study and research at Mansfield College, just as Adam had done. Fittingly, we hope to be welcoming the first Adam von Trott Scholar to Mansfield in the academic year 2009–10, which also marks the centenary of Adam's birth.

Dr Diana Walford CBE
April 2008

Foreword by David Marquand
Former Principal of Mansfield College

The great American historian, John Lukacs, dedicated his path-breaking study of the 'duel' between Hitler and Churchill to the memory of two people. One was Brigadier Claude Nicholson, 'defender of British honour at Calais'. (Nicholson had commanded the British forces during the German siege of Calais in May 1940.) The other was Adam von Trott zu Solz, 'defender of German honour in Berlin'. There is no doubt that Lukacs' tribute was deserved. Von Trott and his colleagues did seek to defend German honour. Indeed, they tried to save it from the evil embrace of National Socialism. The failure of their famous 1944 July Plot to assassinate Hitler does not detract from the moral significance of their endeavour. They wanted to show that Hitler's Germany was not the only one: that there was another Germany that rejected the barbaric savagery of the Nazis to which too many Germans had closed their eyes, and that remained true to the fundamental values of human dignity, justice, responsibility and self respect. They also wanted to show that denizens of that other Germany were prepared, if necessary, to die for their beliefs.

All this, they did. As Joachim Fest, the leading historian of the German resistance put it, the July 20 assassination attempt was 'primarily a symbolic act'; its purpose was 'the gesture itself; it was its own justification'.[1] But, as Fest also points out, there was a hideous irony here. Von Trott and his fellow plotters were isolated, not just from the Nazi true believers, but from the great mass of the German people. Hitler had never won an absolute majority in a free election, but his diplomatic triumphs in the 1930s had carried him to undreamed of heights of popularity. Even some of the eventual plotters supported him before the war, and in some cases in its early stages. We cannot know with any certainty how ordinary Germans saw the plot and the plotters after its failure. (They were not, of course, aware of it before then.) It was dangerous to express

Foreword by David Marquand

hostility to the regime in public places, and intelligence reports on popular attitudes are necessarily unreliable. That said, the evidence suggests that, if anything, the bomb plot and its failure boosted Hitler's popularity, at least for a while, and that, to quote Fest again, the masses 'still had a dark, fatalistic feeling that their destiny was inextricably bound up with his'.[2]

Even after the war, German attitudes were, at best, ambivalent. For many on the left, von Trott and his fellow conspirators were too aristocratic, too much part of a remote, upper-class elite, to make congenial heroes. To many on the right, they seemed at least faintly unpatriotic; to a few they seemed downright treacherous. The other Germany that the plotters hoped to embody emerged, dazed and in some cases traumatised, from the ruins of wartime destruction, and in a surprisingly short time it flourished as never before. It was incorporated into the western alliance, and played a crucial role in setting up the European Community that eventually became the European Union. Democratic institutions and – more importantly – democratic values are now embedded in Germany's political culture life at least as firmly as in those of France, Britain or the United States. Old notions of a German *Sonderweg*, or special path, embodying uniquely German and quintessentially undemocratic values, have vanished, virtually without trace. Today, Germany is more often criticised for her unwillingness to engage in military activities beyond her borders than for incorrigible and dangerous militarism. The demons of Germany's past – not just those of the Nazi era but those of earlier times – have been laid to rest. She has become a model democracy and a model civilian power.

But the harsh truth is that the exemplary courage and nobility of spirit displayed by von Trott and his associates played virtually no part in this process. Post-war Germany has been a democratic and pacific nation, but its constitution and political culture have little in common with the dreams of the Kreisau Circle. It is a federal state, but it was not built from the bottom up by small, self-governing communities, as the Kreisauers wanted. It was built from the top down, to a large extent by the western allies. By the same token, the present-day European Union is far from the bottom-up federation that von Trott and his colleagues hoped to see. On a deeper level, the Kreisauers loathing for, and fear of, mass society, of which they saw Nazism as an emanation, has had little purchase in the post-war world, with its rampant consumerism and hyper-individualism. The generation of Germans that rebuilt their country in the post-war years, and whose monument is the pacific and successful Germany of today, did not see von Trott and his associates as spiritual guides or political mentors. They were too busy with the mundane task of rebuilding.

An even crueller irony is that it is not at all clear that if the plot had succeeded, and Hitler had been killed, the allies would have been willing to negotiate with the new regime – or, for that matter, that the German people would have rallied to it. By July 1944, with the Red Army racing through eastern Europe, British and American bombers pounding German cities with impunity, and British and American armies fighting in Normandy, it was obvious to allied policy makers that Germany's defeat was only a matter of time. 'Unconditional Surrender' had become their mantra; and they might well have continued to insist on it. A post-plot German Government that accepted the allies' terms – as a post-plot German Government would have had to do – might have furnished the basis for a new version of the 'stab in the back' myth that dogged the Weimar Republic, and became a favourite trope of Hitler's rhetoric.

But none of this really matters. Von Trott and the other members of the German Resistance should not be judged by a utilitarian calculus. They did what they did, not because they thought it would produce this or that result, still less because they had weighed the odds, but because, like Martin Luther, they could do no other. That is why their memory speaks to us through the fog of the most terrible war, and the most evil regime, in human history. In the end, that is all that can be said. It ought to be enough.

Notes
1. Joachim Fest (translated by Bruce Little), *Plotting Hitler's Death: The German Resistance to Hitler, 1933–1945* (Weidenfeld and Nicolson, London, 1996), p. 340.
2. Ibid., p. 321.

List of Illustrations

Illustrations are placed after page 46.
1 Adam vot Trott in 1932.
2 Count Helmuth James von Moltke, leader of the Kreisau Circle, on trial in the People's Court, January 1945.
3 General Ludwig Beck, Chief of Army General Staff, 1935–38. He became leader of Resistance in the Armed Forces. He was designated Head of State if the 1944 plot had been successful.
4 Colonel Claus Schenk Graf von Stauffenberg (extreme left) standing to attention next to General Friedrich Fromm who is being greeted on arrival at the Wolfsschanze (Wolf's Lair) on 15 July 1944. On Hitler's left, holding a folder, is Field Marshal Wilhelm Keitel, Head of Overall High Command of the Armed Forces.
5 The conference room at the Wolfsschanze after the assassination attempt, 20 July 1944.
6 Adam von Trott, about 1935.
7 Adam's mother, Eleonore von Trott zu Solz (born von Schweinitz).
8 Adam von Trott as a young student.
9 Adam with his father.
10 Adam in Oxford.
11 Adam von Trott, about 1935.
12 Adam von Trott at Cliveden with David Astor.
13 Adam at a conference of the Institute of Pacific Relations, November 1939 (front row, 2nd from right).
14 In Davos, March 1942.
15 Adam during a wartime visit to Basle, autumn 1943.
16 Johannes Winkelmann, Adam von Trott, Peter Bielenberg, summer 1939.
17 Family group at Imshausen, 1944.
18 Hans-Bernd von Haeften on trial in the People's Court. Adam in background.
19 & 20 Adam on trial in the *Volksgerichtshof* (People's Court), 15 August 1944.

List of Illustrations

21 Memorial stone for Adam von Trott zu Solz and his friends, overlooking Imshausen. The inscription reads – Adam von Trott zu Solz 9.8.1909– 26.8.1944. Executed with his friends in the struggle against the destroyers of our homeland. Pray for them. Heed their example.
22 Adam on trial in the *Volksgerichtshof* (People's Court), 15 August 1944.
23 Memorial cross, visible for many miles, on the hill above Imshausen.
24 With Foreign Office colleagues Alexander Worth, Hans Felix Richter, Josias von Rantzau.
25 Wilfrid Israel, Anglo-German, general manager of family department store in Berlin. He travelled freely on his British passport and was able to get many Jews out of Germany. Close friend of Adam.
26 The Rt. Revd. G.K.A. Bell, Bishop of Chichester, close friend of Dietrich Bonhoeffer.
27 With Foreign Office colleagues Hans Felix Richter, Trump, Alexander Worth, Leipholdt.
28 In the uniform of his student corps at Göttingen University.
29 Colonel Claus Schenk Graf von Stauffenberg, who planted the bomb in the conference room at the Wolfsschanze, 20 July 1944.
30 Major-General Henning von Tresckow, leader of resistance on the Eastern front; photograph taken a few days before he took his own life on 21 July 1944. He planted a bomb on Hitler's aeroplane in 1943, but it failed to explode.
31 General Franz Halder, Chief of Army General Staff, 1938–42, leader of the planned Army coup in September 1938.
32 The Revd. Dr W.B. Selbie, Principal of Mansfield College, who brought Adam to Oxford in 1929.
33 Dr Carl Goerdler, former Mayor of Leipzig. He was to become Chancellor-Elect if the 1944 coup had been successful.
34 Dietrich Bonhoeffer, Evangelical pastor and theologian, university chaplain in Berlin, pastoral posts in Spain and London. Worked closely with the Abwehr and resistance groups.
35 Adam and Clarita von Trott.
36 Otto John (with his brother Hans on right). Lawyer at Lufthansa and linked to the Foreign Office resistance group.
37 Field Marshal Erwin von Witzleben who would have seized Government offices and arrested Hitler if the planned 1938 coup had been successful. Later designated to be Commander-in-Chief of the Army if the 1944 plot had been successful.
38 Ulrich von Hassell in the People's Court. Former ambassador in Rome. Key member of Beck–Goerdler section of resistance.

List of Illustrations

39 Postcard sent to Charles Collins by Adam von Trott at Christmas 1933, eleven months after the Nazis came to power, in which he refers to "changes in the world's bigger scenarios".
40 Imshausen, the von Trott family home.
41 Adam von Trott with Charles Collins and an estate forester at Imshausen, 1932.

1
Early Years

Adam von Trott zu Solz was born on 9 August 1909 in Potsdam, the capital of the province of Brandenburg. His father's family had been resident in Hesse since the Middle Ages and, in addition to running their estates, had been prominent in the public life of Hesse, and later Germany, for four hundred years. His mother was of the Schweinitz family; and it was here that there was an interesting American connection. Adam's maternal grandfather, Lothar von Schweinitz, became Prussian ambassador in Vienna after the 1866 Austro-Prussian war, remaining there for ten years. He formed a close friendship with the American ambassador, John Jay, who was the grandson of John Jay, friend of Washington and first Chief Justice of the United States. Von Schweinitz, at the age of 50, married the 23 years old daughter of his American colleague. Their second child, Eleonore, was Adam's mother. Adam was therefore the great, great, great grandson of the first Chief Justice of the United States.

Although Eleonore saw herself as a German national and loyally carried out all the functions of the wife of a senior Prussian official, she always remembered her American inheritance and the part the Jay family played in the abolition of slavery. She was deeply religious and was prominent in the ecumenical movement, speaking out boldly against any restriction of human rights. The American ancestry and his mother's ecumenism were important strands in the moulding of Adam's character and outlook, for he saw himself as a citizen not just of Germany, but of the wider Western world; and his mother's religious contacts were to lead eventually to his arrival at Mansfield College, Oxford, and through that experience, to his later Rhodes Scholarship at Balliol College and his close involvement with the British political scene.

Adam's early education in Potsdam came from his nurse, an Englishwoman named Louisa Barrett, to whom he became very devoted. In later life he often spoke of her with emotion, saying how much she had meant to him in his early life. He had only one criticism – her

German pronunciation when she read him his nightly fairy tale. When, many years later, she was retired and living in a country cottage in England, he always went to see her on his visits to this country. In 1914, when he was five years old, she had to leave the family service and Adam started to attend school in Berlin. He remained there for two years, but when the family moved from Berlin in 1917 he attended a school in Kassel. He then studied at the family home, Imshausen (a late 18th century country house built on the site of an ancient Trott castle), followed by four years at a boarding school in Hannoversch-Munden, passing his Abitur in 1927. Although he was not happy at boarding school, he could sometimes remember the days nostalgically; sixteen years later, during the Allied air raids on Berlin in November and December 1943, he wrote to his wife:

> Yesterday as I was salvaging things in the Kurfurstenstrasse, I found as I flashed my torch over the walls of a dark room, a very pretty old-fashioned painting of Hannoversch-Munden, done in the manner of Merian but bigger and more naïve. In that strange moment it brought back to me the memory of the lovely, half-obscure, half-threatening, half-simple-minded years of my boyhood in that town, embedded in huge forests and valleys which I will show you one day. There too I loved life in a way and was sometimes very happy.[1]

When he was only nine years old, the First World War ended and the remainder of his schoolboy years were spent in the aftermath of the catastrophe that had overtaken the world and particularly Europe. Nearly nine million men had been killed, nearly two million of them from Germany. In addition, countless numbers suffered for the rest of their lives from shell shock and the effects of gas as they struggled through the days of world depression to raise a new generation which, hopefully, would not have to experience war in their lifetime. In parts of the Western Front, the once fertile fields had become a desolate wasteland; and only the debris of war and the crosses that stood like sentinels in the silence could speak of the suffering of a generation of men whose experience could never adequately be expressed in words. In many homesteads throughout Germany, as in other countries, families had to come to terms with the knowledge that a son, or a husband, or a father would not come home and the framed photograph or the portrait on the wall would have to serve as the reminder of happy laughter and love in days gone by. A way of life had gone for ever and a stunned continent would now have to pick up the pieces and try to mould them into something new. It was in this changed Europe that Adam, with his deep intellect and his family tradition of public service, would have to take his place.

2
University Life – Munich and Göttingen

In May 1927 Adam matriculated at the University of Munich. He was to read law and public administration, thus preparing himself for life as a public servant. He had no marked political leanings at that time, but one evening he and some students attended a meeting of one of the fringe right-wing parties which were fairly numerous in Bavaria, the difference being that this one already had a few representatives in the Reichstag. The meeting was addressed by a leader who was well-known in Munich for his Austrian accent and his small moustache. He was Adolf Hitler. Adam was impressed by his verbal energy, but otherwise the meeting seems to have had little effect on him. At the end of term he left for Vienna and Budapest, returning home in July. Under the German university system, it was possible for students, having completed a semester in one university, to move on to another; and he therefore decided not to return to Munich, but to transfer to the University of Göttingen. One of his close friends from those days, Ernst Friedemann Freiherr von Munchhausen, recalled after the war the striking appearance of Adam during his first Göttingen semester in 1927:

> Under the high forehead and heavy eyebrows were dark blue eyes with an expression which at the same time brought forth the clear depth of understanding and showed the compelling force of feeling . . . whoever met him once felt that he was one of those gifted persons that one only seldom meets.[2]

In the summer of 1928 Adam attended a meeting in Geneva that was to be of enormous significance in his life. During the summer of 1927 his mother, who with her strong puritanical strain was a member of several religious bodies, attended an international conference for church youth leaders at Dassel in Hanover, while Adam was travelling in Eastern

Europe. During the conference she met three church leaders then based in Geneva, the Revd Tracy Strong, Dr W. A. Visser't Hooft of the World Alliance of YMCAs and Robert Abernathy. At her request, Tracy Strong arranged for Adam to spend part of his 1928 vacation in Geneva. On 20th September of that year, he visited Visser't Hooft for the first time; in his 'Memoirs' published in 1973 Visser't Hooft wrote:

> In 1928 when he was nineteen years old Adam spent a holiday in Geneva and visited us several times. I felt strongly attracted to this very bright student who was so keenly aware of the perilous and tragic situation of the younger generation in Germany in the spiritual confusion after the first world war. His good looks, his tall figure, his high forehead gave him the appearance of the perfect aristocrat. But in his conversation he showed the humility of a young man desperately anxious to find some stable foundation for his life.[3]

Whilst in Geneva Adam was introduced by Tracy Strong to Conrad Hoffman, Director of European Student Relief for the World Student Christian Association, who arranged for him to attend a SCM conference in Liverpool from 2nd to 8th of January 1929. In the autumn term 1928 he fell ill at Göttingen and had to return to Imshausen for convalescence. However, he was well enough to go to Liverpool for the conference in January, the theme of which was 'The Purpose of God in the Life of the World'. He took the conference in his stride and made contacts and friends who would be useful in the future. Among them were Prof. W. G. Adams, Warden of All Souls College, and G. J. Scholten, a Dutch student who during the war was to provide a valuable link with the Dutch resistance. Already he was hoping to spend a term at Oxford and during the conference he was introduced to the Revd Dr W. B. Selbie.

William Boothby Selbie enrolled as the first student of Mansfield College in 1886, having taken a degree in Literae Humaniores at Brasenose. After pastorates at Highgate and Cambridge, he became Principal of Mansfield in 1909, just nine weeks after Adam was born. In 1920 he became the first Free Churchman since the time of Cromwell to receive an Oxford DD. His son, Lt R. J. Selbie, was killed whilst serving with the Quebec Regiment in June 1916 and is buried in Hooge Crater Military Cemetery, Ypres. Dr Selbie died in April 1944 and thus did not know of the tragic death of his German student four months later.

Apart from being a leading scholar of German theology, and the author of a book on Schleiermacher, Dr Selbie was a friend of the theologian Adolf von Harnack who had founded the Kaiser Wilhelm Society for the Advancement of Science with the help of Adam's father when the latter was Minister of Culture and Education in the Prussian Government. Dr Selbie was impressed with the young German student and invited him to spend a term at Mansfield. Adam accepted eagerly and, after a short break at home, he returned to England in January 1929.

3
Mansfield College

After spending a few days in London at the home of his aunt, Mrs Beatrix de Candole, Adam arrived at Mansfield on Sunday, 20 January 1929. The next day he wrote his first letter to his father from Oxford. The letter is movingly interesting from two aspects – like most students writing to their parents, he dwells on the practical aspects, not least his finances; and he shows a courteous respect and warmth of feeling towards Dr Selbie. The letter gives the impression of a polite, dedicated young man. The full text of the letter is:

> OXFORD. MANSFIELD COLLEGE.
> *21.1.28 (a mistake for 1929)*

Dear Father,
This letter must be in answer to mother's as well as reporting to you both about my new circumstances. As a matter of fact Aunt Beatrix has given me £5; I went with it to a famous shop which buys from high class tailors dress suits which have been returned by their customers for some trifling reasons. However I found no good evening suit there for less than £10 – but at this price one which fits excellently. Aunt Maria offered me the remaining £5 as a long-term loan – that means giving me credit until March – and as I dare to assume that you would repay her the 100 marks for a really good dress suit, once the major pressure of your expenses for me are behind you – I accepted the kind offer!?

As for me here in Oxford, I do really hope to manage within my allowance. With free meals (lunch and dinner) I pay 25/- [shillings] a week, which is a thoroughly practicable figure as long as no unexpectedly high incidental expenses arise. I should, however, be grateful if I could receive my allowance a little earlier, best by registered post, so that I can pay everything at once.

Dr Selbie, the Principal of Mansfield, is one of England's best known theologians and a prominent leader amongst the Free Churches. He is very kind, and to save me the expensive cost of living outside college, he has lodged me in the guest room; and he has been specially concerned about my studies. For example, he has arranged that I may attend certain lectures in the area of national politics, which are of great interest to me. The only disadvantage is that my room is huge and so almost impossible to heat (for example, at the moment I have quite stiff fingers!) The college has about 60 members and is a modern building which on the one hand provides ample space and on the other skilfully follows the splendid architecture of Oxford.

It is certainly not all that easy, being in every respect a stranger/foreigner here, to adapt and settle in – nevertheless, it will be all right!

Apart from attending lectures (in politics as well as in theology) and having tutorials with Dr Selbie, Adam entered fully into the life of Mansfield. On Sunday mornings he attended service in chapel with the other students. John Marsh, who was a student at the time and was later to be Principal of the college, was very friendly with him and wrote in 1989:

> I saw more of him, I think, than did any other Mansfield man. I liked him immensely . . . He was a great fellow and I recall his own calculation about the 'rightness' of a conspiracy to take a man's life – even if the man was Hitler.[4]

This is an interesting statement, because it indicates the probability that Adam and John Marsh were in touch with each other in later years. Hitler did not come to power until 1933, four years after Adam and John Marsh were at Mansfield together; and in 1929 there were very few people in Germany or elsewhere who regarded him seriously. It must have been some years later that Adam communicated his views to John, possibly during his visits to Oxford in 1939, by which time John Marsh was back in Mansfield as Chaplain and Tutor.

The winter of 1928–1929 was a particularly severe one and it is not surprising that Adam comments to his parents about the coldness of his room. Living in a room where the temperature was never above 46°F, it was not surprising that he thought of his warm Imshausen 'with a certain envy'.

In another letter he again shows his appreciation of those who have made it possible for him to go to Mansfield:

The secretary (Miss Read) of the Student Christian Movement is the person to whom I am indebted most of all. Not only because she has achieved Oxford for me, and also a few days in London staying with some extremely nice people, but she continues to be concerned that I make contact with people here who are interesting and useful to me.

Dr Selbie is a really extraordinary man. His nickname here in Oxford is 'The inspired mouse' – he is very small and also quite stooped and already fairly old. He is a friend of Harnack, etc. Despite his typical English reserve and taciturn nature he takes a great interest in me, which could well be due to his partiality for everything German.

In addition to experiencing life at Mansfield, he explored the city – 'The town is strikingly beautiful and each day one can admire new beauties' he wrote to his father. On February 10th he wrote separately to both his father and mother, giving something of his impression of Mansfield and Oxford:

> OXFORD. MANSFIELD COLLEGE
> *10.ii.28 (a mistake for 1929)*

My dear Father,
For some unknown reason the days here pass more quickly than elsewhere, without anything getting done – yet it is indeed difficult to summarise on paper the essence of these days . . . In Mansfield College people are very friendly, and this is also true of Dr Selbie who is a wise and clever man, eminent in his own field. Curiously enough the people with whom I get along best are the Americans. The town itself is strikingly beautiful and each day one can admire new beauties, yet nevertheless not feel really at home. The education which the English receive here, and indeed have done for 500 years, is notably different from ours. Possibly the most characteristic factor is that everything is in the setting of a national and conservative background. Interest in politics is exceptionally strong and at the moment is particularly concerned with the very acute social and economic difficulties. A splendidly developed quality in England is the ability to compromise. The average 'intellectual' level of the students is probably lower than ours. On the other hand there is the practical side of the English, evident also amongst students, who would never start on something which they will not later be able to use, and they have a pretty eye for positive and negative movements in political and church life.

Aunt Beatrix is coming by car from London today to visit me. She is very nice to me . . . Many thanks, by the way, for the money which I neglected to confirm.

Your faithful son
Adam

P.S. Please give mother my warmest greetings – I thank her very much for her letter and I wait daily for her next one!!! I have written to Werner [his brother] and also await reply.

Extract from a letter to his mother, dated 10 February 1929:

I have met some very unpleasant German students here who have a lot of money and are playing a very nasty role – they have founded a 'German Club' in which are also very many Englishmen and it isn't all that easy to avoid them. It is embarrassingly shameful to have to witness their behaviour without having any influence on them.

Tomorrow is Ulla's and today is Ella's birthday – all the best to both of them – I wrote to Werner many days ago and long for his reply.
I think of the warm Imshausen with a certain envy – my room here has, I think, never had a temperature above 8° Celsius, so it takes quite some energy to hold the pen in half-frozen fingers so that the result is legible.

I find that our letters take a long time to arrive, which means that you and I should not allow too long to elapse before answering . . . My return occurs at the end of March . . . Now, goodbye – and please, away with this letter, for it's indeed only a tiny excerpt! Greetings to Father!

Yours   *Adam*

He made a few other friends in the university, one of whom, Geoffrey Wilson, he had met in Geneva the previous year. Wilson was an undergraduate at Oriel and they now explored Oxford together and forged a friendship which lasted until the war. In the spring of 1939, Wilson visited Imshausen and Adam then took him on a tour via Heidelberg, Munich and Berlin to meet people opposed to the Nazi regime. During this journey he outlined to Wilson, who was then secretary to Stafford Cripps, his ideas on how Hitler could be removed.

Shortly before term ended he wrote a letter home in which he briefly summarized his thoughts on his Mansfield studies. In his earlier letter written on 10th February to his mother, he had expressed some personal doubt as to whether he had been able 'to make much of the brilliant possibilities open to me here . . . in consequence of too little learning'. Now, in his final letter, his confidence returned:

. . . always to remain aware that I am a foreigner and a German and so from a particular standpoint can choose good from bad. Nevertheless, if I have succeeded more and more in living to some extent as an Englishman among Englishmen, that is, in not being conspicuous, that was for me a good policy for me to follow here.

So far as my studies here are concerned, I can sum up by saying that the theological lectures have given me rather more stimulation than perhaps needless headaches, but on the whole a quite comprehensive glimpse of this quite 'other' world. Dr Selbie and the personal/private conversations with him have been the most valuable of all. The political science lectures were of great value to me. As is the custom here, after a time I went to the professor and asked whether I might put some particular questions to him.

In the *Mansfield College Magazine* for July 1929 the Junior Common Room President, R. L. Franks, wrote:

During the Hilary Term we greatly enjoyed the presence and companionship of the Baron von Trott zu Solz (to give him his full title, though he was affectionately known at 'Trotsky'), a German law student who came to this country for the Liverpool Quadrennial SCM Conference, and who wished to learn something of the ways of English theological colleges. He was a great asset to the life of the college, and those who lived in college especially were refreshed and cheered by his amazing and amusing personality. We were sorry he could only stay amongst us for one term.

When he left Mansfield at the end of Hilary Term, Adam had already decided that this was not to be the end of his association with Oxford. Indeed, Mansfield had opened for him a window on to a university life which was much different from the one he had known in Germany, and one to which his character and outlook were in many ways more suited. In Göttingen much of student life, as in other German universities, centred round the Student Corps; and he played his part well in his corps and maintained contact with corps members through the years. In Oxford, however, he had seen a different kind of student life, where young people gathered in to groups and societies which often had little or no formal structure, drawn together only by their shared intellectual interests.

It was therefore with a new insight into university life that Adam journeyed from Mansfield to London to spend a few days with his aunt, Mrs

Beatrix de Candole, who like him was descended from John Jay. From there he went to Holland to see his new friend Scholten and to attend a meeting of the World Student Movement and then on to his parents at Imshausen.

Immediately on his return home, he wrote an essay of 4,000 words entitled 'Impressions of a German student in England', attempting to analyse the differences between the German and British post-war student generations. He saw his German fellow-students as 'lost in the bewildering mazes of the world of thought', whilst British students could formulate objectives and translate their energies into action. At the end of this essay, which is in the archives at Imshausen, he emphasizes his thanks to Dr Selbie:

> I have to emphasise especially in conclusion what I wanted to express through all this, namely my sincerest thanks to the British Student Christian Movement and to Dr Selbie, to whom I owe this opportunity for a time which meant to me personally such a lot, and is perhaps one more step to international friendship and understanding.

Clarita von Trott has recently said that she remembers that he was happy about the tutorial work that he did at Mansfield and later built upon; also that he studied some subjects with Dr Selbie himself. She adds – 'Without this experience he might not perhaps have been so determined to achieve a Rhodes Scholarship'.[5] It is interesting that he continued to speak of his Mansfield experience so many years after being there; it was obviously a very formative time in his life.

4

University Life – Göttingen and Berlin

In May 1929 Adam formally ex-matriculated from Göttingen and entered the law faculty at Berlin University, living for a time with his uncle Ebehard von Schweinitz in the Kaiser's former palace in central Berlin. From there he moved to a room in the Pariserstrasse.

At about this time he became friendly with Hugh Montgomery, a third secretary at the British Embassy in Berlin; and possibly through him he met Albrecht von Kessel, a junior official in the Ministry of Foreign Affairs. They became firm friends and shared their opposition to the Nazis, although Kessel was the more fortunate because in 1944 he was serving in the German Embassy in Italy and survived the war. Kessel described Adam's room in the Pariserstrasse: 'cheap and gloomy digs, on the sole wobbly table of which were arranged in a truly artistic still life, Marx's Das Capital, Holderlin's poems, a hairbrush, and a slice of bread and butter'.[6]

In Berlin, he developed his contacts with working-class and socialist groups and wrote to his father that he believed himself 'finally to be on the right track'. He saw the positive side of socialism, but was never attracted to Marxism – 'I am constantly impressed by the under-estimation in Socialist (especially Marxist) circles of the values which form personality and create friendly co-operation'. He found Marxism to be too rigid and socially devisive a doctrine for dealing with the practical and political problems of life.

In late spring 1930 he returned to Göttingen and in August became eligible to vote when he achieved his age majority. The following month, with the Weimar Republic on the brink of collapse because of the economic crisis, and with unemployment in Germany at over six million, Chancellor Brüning called elections to give him a clear mandate to govern. Adam, having moved to the left in the past year, voted for the

Social Democratic party. After the election they were still the strongest party in the Reichstag, but there were substantial gains by the Communists and the National Socialists (Nazis). With 107 seats the Nazis were the second largest party in the assembly; by parliamentary means, Hitler had reached the last phase of his struggle to control Germany. The events which were to lead to the tragic ending of Adam's short life had been set firmly in train.

He took his Referendar examinations in November and December 1930 and was judged volbefriedigend (fully satisfactory); he was now a probationer counsel. Normally he would have proceeded to complete the second part after three years service in the courts, to enable him to practise at the bar, but instead he elected to submit a doctoral dissertation. On 18 July 1931 the thesis was accepted and marked *summa cum laude*, the highest distinction possible.

One reason for completing his dissertation quickly can be traced back to his time at Mansfield. He was so impressed by Oxford that he decided, whilst still at Mansfield, that he would like to return to the university at some time to take a degree course. A route suggested to him was that of the Rhodes Scholarship scheme. Among those who had been among the first group of Rhodes Scholars in 1903 was his uncle, Ebehard von Schweinitz. No scholarships had been awarded to Germans since 1913, but the practice was revived in 1930 (although limited to two each year) when Fritz Schumacher and William Koelle went up to Oxford. In the same year, Adam's uncle encouraged him to apply. Six referees were required and he chose three from among his Göttingen teachers, the others being Ebehard von Schweinitz, Dr Selbie and A. L. Rowse. The latter was only a young Oxford don at the time and it is safe to assume that the German selection committee were principally impressed by the testimonials of von Schweinitz and the Principal of Mansfield College. Adam expressed a preference for Balliol, because it was his uncle's college and also because he understood it to have a reputation for being politically progressive. He wanted to have senior student status at Oxford, in order to take the degree course in two years instead of three, and the university required the doctorate in order to grant such status. In January 1931 he appeared before the Rhodes Selection Committee in Berlin and on the 9th of January he was notified that he had been awarded a Rhodes Scholarship.

5

Rhodes Scholar

Adam arrived to take up his Rhodes Scholarship at Balliol, reading Philosophy, Politics and Economics (PPE), in Michaelmas Term 1931. Arriving in England, he travelled from London to Oxford by bus and on 10th October wrote to his parents:

> By and large I do not think it will be difficult for me to find my feet again in Oxford. It is not so much a question of reliving old impressions as of changing oneself. . . . When I first saw Magdalén Tower again from a bus coming from London my feelings were almost overwhelming. The tender emotion that one has towards this architecture is not mere sentimentality.

It had been a very damp and dismal autumn that year; it was as if the weather was a precursor to the clouds of unrest and doubt and war which were progressively to envelop Europe in the coming decade. In the 1920s all had seemed set fair for a peaceful and prosperous future as new generations of students enjoyed university life freed from the restraints and trauma of war. From the late 1920s onwards, however, Oxford was changing. The economic collapse, leading to mass unemployment, the dole queues and the industrial wastelands, brought a greater social awareness to many Oxford students and a general swing to the left in their political outlook. The rise of the dictators sharpened political attitudes further and the fun and the frivolity of the twenties steadily gave way to a more sober and serious mood. It was a time of transition.

One of Adam's greatest attributes, acknowledged by all who knew him, was his loyalty to his friends. Once he had formed a friendship, he would keep it and take it up at later stages in life. Thus it was not surprising that, as soon as he returned to Oxford, he resumed his friendship with Dr Selbie – although it had never lapsed, as is witnessed by the fact that Dr Selbie was one of his referees for his Rhodes Scholarship. In view of the proximity of Rhodes House to Mansfield, it would be natural for him to call in at Mansfield, bearing in mind the strong place it held in his affections and memory. Dr Selbie was by then not in too good health, but on his retirement from Mansfield a year later, he and Mrs Selbie moved to 174 Banbury Road where it was easy for Adam to visit them.

He quickly formed new friendships. The Master of Balliol, A. D. Lindsay, took a particular interest in him and the friendship between them lasted to the end; even during the war Adam was able to keep in touch with friends in Oxford and elsewhere through connections in neutral countries. Isaiah Berlin was another friend who in 1984 recalled their first meeting:

> We met at lunch . . . at the end of which he suggested that we might go for a walk that afternoon. We became friends almost at once. He had exceptional charm, great distinction of mind and manner, was extremely handsome, had both wit and humour, and was at all times, a most delightful companion. I was completely captivated. He had a far wider view of history and culture than most of my Oxford friends.

There were, however, some people with whom he formed particularly close friendships. David Astor met Adam in the porter's lodge on his first day at Balliol. They were immediately drawn to each other and Adam became probably the most influential single person in David Astor's life. Later, when so many of Adam's friends deserted him and failed to support him when he needed it most, he defended him against all attacks and, after the war ended, worked tirelessly to honour his memory and pursue the ideals that were Adam's lifeblood.

Two close friendships were with Sheila Grant Duff and Diana Hubback; the two girls had been at school together before going to Oxford and were close friends. They both visited him and his parents at Imshausen. After leaving Oxford, Adam and Sheila Grant Duff corresponded regularly – sometimes twice a week – until war broke out in 1939. They pledged themselves to form 'the best friendship in Europe'. Over 300 of the letters they wrote to each other between 1932 and 1939 survived; they are the record not just of a tender and loving friendship, but of the political and international tensions of the 1930s as Europe moved forward inexorably towards the abyss.

He also corresponded with Diana Hubback and, as with Sheila Grant Duff, they met from time to time. His letters to her continued until 1942, when in March he wrote – 'We think and talk of you often and hope that, in spite of all, there remains at heart a realm of peace in which one day we may meet again.'[7]

His other close Balliol friend was Charles Collins who later joined the Foreign Office. Adam's fate had a profound effect on Collins which lasted for the rest of his life; and ordinary occurrences of life would often prompt him to a quiet comment – whenever he heard Beethoven's 5th (Emperor) Piano Concerto, he would remark 'That was one of Adam von Trott's favourite pieces of music'. In November 1946 he wrote 'Notes on Adam von Trott' for Adam's children, in which he recalled that Adam 'was never unmindful of the real business of his life which was the future of Germany' and 'he knew that even in the most favourable circumstances that future would be difficult; he feared that it would be tragic'.[8]

Apart from his PPE studies, Adam involved himself in political circles, having taken upon himself the duty of improving relations between Germany and Britain. In his first month at Balliol he spoke in the German Club about his distaste of National Socialism, whilst at the same time speaking up for what he considered the legitimate rights of his own country and the righting of the wrongs of the Treaty of Versailles. Continually he tried to distinguish between Germany as a nation and National Socialism as a cult which had taken it over.

It was in the Oxford evening paper in Balliol College JCR that he read on 30 January 1933 that the ailing President von Hindenburg had appointed Hitler as Chancellor. Charles Collins recalled later:

> He knew at once that a terrible disaster had befallen his country; that the prospects for his own future had undergone a fundamental change; that it was a future in which a bitter struggle would be needed to achieve even the smallest result; that many of his friends and acquaintances were at once in personal danger. A number of things he was sure of immediately; that overt opposition to the new regime would be useless for a long time to come; that nevertheless he must oppose it by all the means in his power; that a common ground must be found for as many opponents of the regime as possible, and that he himself would try to find that ground in a struggle for the 'liberal' rights; that, although it would certainly be at the cost of handicap to his own career he would not join the Nazi party unless it should ever become his clear duty to do so in furtherance of his anti-Nazi activity. All these things he expressed to me on the same night that he learned of Hitler's coming to power.[9]

He still had two more terms to run at Oxford. Increasingly he found it difficult to conceal his anxiety about Germany's ultimate fate. His concern about the future, and the role that he himself would play in it, placed him apart from his more carefree contemporaries. In Trinity Term he was working hard for his Schools (final examinations). At a party Isaiah Berlin heard him say to someone, 'My country is very sick'.[10] It was said that he was thinking of joining the German army, believing that the General Staff was now the only institution that could remove Hitler. He said to Professor Brock of Cambridge, 'I don't know which is the more difficult at the moment for a good German, whether to remain in Germany or to stay abroad. In the one it will be sour, in the other bitter'.[11] He hoped he might get a fellowship at All Souls College, for which he would normally need a first-class honours. Between Schools and his viva voce on 25 July, he wrote to his father about the Oxford he was about to leave:

> I returned here yesterday. Most of the undergraduates have gone down, and Oxford is of an almost miraculous beauty in its summer stillness. It has given me more than perhaps I shall ever be able to tell. Europe's noblest traditions live on here, hardly noticeably, unconsciously, kept alive by a race which is simple and genuinely political. But about that let us speak more later.

When he received a second-class honours he was very disappointed. Diana Hubback walked with him in Hyde Park on the night the results were published – 'there was no way to comfort him'.[12] He still hoped he might get the fellowship, but in the event All Souls did not elect anyone that autumn.

At the beginning of August 1933 Adam sailed from Southampton to Hamburg. The Oxford experience, which had started with such excitement and enthusiasm at Mansfield four years earlier, had ended with a degree of disappointment. But there was solace in a valedictory letter from his friend Christopher Cox at New College:

> There are few undergraduates (if I may say so!) in the last seven years who have contributed as much intellectually and culturally as well as socially to Oxford as you have done; and no one could have vindicated more triumphantly the revival of the German Rhodes Scholarships. To that the accident of a second makes no difference.[13]

6
The Years 1933–1936

The next three years were spent in completing Adam's legal training. He worked in various courts, but consistently refused to join the Nazi party. Increasingly he was worried by the attitude of so many of his Oxford friends who took the view that because he had returned to Germany, he must be sympathetic to the Nazi regime. On the 22nd and 23rd of January 1934 the *Manchester Guardian* published articles on the persecution of the Jews by the Nazis, with special reference to Hesse. Adam felt the newspaper was encouraging international hatred and wrote a reply in which he said that from his own experience, there was little anti-Semitism in the Hessian courts. It was published on 21st February with a rejoinder by the author of the articles. A lively correspondence ensued, opening with a letter on 5th March from Dr Selbie. He wrote that his attention had been called to the letter and the rejoinder; and he continued:

> I hope that it is not too late to assure you and your readers that Mr von Trott is by no means the blind and prejudiced reporter he (the special correspondent) imagines him to be. I knew Mr von Trott well when he was recently a Rhodes scholar at Balliol, and admired his sound judgement and scrupulous fairness and truthfulness. He is devoted to the task of bringing about a better understanding between his country and our own, and it is most unfortunate that his efforts should be discounted beforehand by the suggestion that he is an untrustworthy witness.
>
> *Yours etc.*   W. B. Selbie[14]

Dr Selbie's reference to the Balliol days clearly indicates that Adam was in close touch with him during those two years.

Although concentrating on building up his legal career, Adam was also consolidating his position as a resister of the Nazi regime. In March 1935 he told his mother in a letter that he wanted 'essential connections' –

people who were likely to rise to positions where they could act effectively against the regime.

In May 1935, after an absence of nearly two years, he returned to England. After a short visit to London, he travelled to Oxford. Most of his undergraduate friends had left Oxford and he therefore moved among the dons with whom he had been friendly. He was disappointed with their coolness towards him; they seemed incapable of understanding that a man could work against National Socialism from within Germany and they increasingly took the view that because he resided and worked in Germany, he must therefore be in sympathy with the aims of the Nazi government.

7

The Far East

By 1936 the Nazi system was so firmly established in Germany that there was no possibility of a popular uprising. Adam felt the need to withdraw for a while in order to view Germany from the outside. He had for long been interested in China and the Far East and now conceived the idea of spending the third year of his Rhodes Scholarship in China. On 8th November 1936 he came to England, staying first in London and then in Oxford. Support for the unusual wish to spend part of a scholarship away from Oxford came from senior academics, including A. D. Lindsay of Balliol, H. A. L. Fisher of New College (who, like Adam, had attended Göttingen University) and E. L. Woodward of Worcester College. Shortly before Christmas he learned that his application had been approved. Early in 1937 he came again to England and on 27th February finally took his B.A. in Oxford. At dinner at All Souls he was introduced to Count Helmuth James von Moltke, who later was to become his firm ally in resistance.

In early March 1937 he left England for America and the Far East, armed with many introductions and a Rhodes Trust grant of £350, as well as personal financial support from Sir Stafford Cripps, who became his closest political friend in Britain. He travelled extensively in the United States and Canada, meeting many influential people in government and political circles as well as his many American cousins. At Harvard he met Felix Frankfurter, who in 1940 was to be the recipient of a letter from R. H. S. Crossman which effectively destabilized Adam in the eyes of the American administration. On 16 July 1937 he boarded a ship for China. As in America, he visited German embassies and offices in China, keeping up the appearance of a loyal citizen of the regime, but this aroused the suspicions of British and American intelligence officers.

Looking back at Europe from the distance of the Far East, he again had to face the choice of whether to pursue his aim of overthrowing the Nazis from within Germany or to move to safer areas from which to carry on his work. However great the temptation to leave Germany permanently, he rejected it every time. He wrote to Sheila Grant Duff from Tsingtao on the 1 October 1938:

> I am strongly tempted to go via America (this entirely between you and myself) to look for a place to work if our continent is really going to be what we both feel threatening now a conflict has been spared. It is a damned hard choice, but I'd rather be a beggar than a slave and I am not too old to start again and I have good friends in America . . . So if things really look safe enough at home, I shall probably proceed to Hongkong and Kunming from Shanghai and there cut across to Rangoon and India. But I shall weigh it very carefully and continue to think about America.[15]

8
Return to Germany and to Resistance

On 28 October 1938 Adam was informed by cable that his father had died of a stroke and he took the next available ship to Europe, the SS Ranchi (P and O). A few days later came the anti-Jewish pogroms of the 9th of November in Germany, kristallnacht, and in a letter written to Diana Hubback in late November, during the voyage home, he expressed his feelings, mentioning a mutual German-Jewish friend, Wilfrid Israel:

> My thoughts have been with him (Wilfrid Israel) very much these last weeks – do you know where he is, how I can reach him? Give him my love if you can. You know that it is we who are humiliated by what has passed and it is for us to wonder whether our former friends wish to have anything more to do with one who, after all (in my case through my very absence) has to accept his full share of responsibility. I know that our friendship is too deeply rooted to be affected by all these developments, but I know of hardly another one I have abroad that in some way or other is not. This I think will be my hardest discovery on returning to Europe after these eventful months. I shall have to face it and set to work in other directions . . . I don't return with any tactics or doctrine but I am determined to hold my own.[16]

Wilfrid Israel was a close friend and supporter of Adam since they met in 1935, 'a wonderfully brave and noble man' as Adam described him in a letter to Diana Hubback. The son of a German father and an English mother, he was the manager of a large family department store in Berlin. Although he held a British passport, he spent two spells in concentration camps. From 1933 to 1939 he was involved in arranging for many Jews, including his own employees, to leave Germany. In 1939 he finally left Germany for London and was employed by the Foreign Research and Press Service in Oxford. At the same time, he continued his work for

Jewish fugitives. In May 1943 he went to Lisbon to help young Jews who had reached Spain and Portugal and to arrange for them to go to Palestine. At the same time, Churchill was in Algiers for talks at General Eisenhower's headquarters. In early June Churchill and Eden flew home via Gibraltar and Lisbon. German agents were following Churchill's movements. As a regular commercial aircraft was about to leave Lisbon, a thickset man sucking a cigar was seen to be walking towards it. Believing the man to be Churchill, a German warplane shot down the defenceless civilian plane. It was the plane on which Israel was travelling and he, together with the other twelve passengers and the crew, were lost. Among the passengers was Leslie Howard, the British actor.

The anti-Jewish pogrom was not popular with the German people and the British chargé d'affaires in Berlin wrote on November 16:

> I have not yet met a single German from any walk of life who does not disapprove to some degree of what has occurred. But I fear that not even the unequivocal condemnation of professed National Socialists and senior officers in the armed forces will have any effect on the gang of madmen who are at present in control in Nazi Germany.[17]

In his diary on 25 November, Ulrich von Hassell, the former German ambassador to Italy, who was to be a leading figure in the resistance, wrote:

> I am writing under the crushing emotions evoked by the vile persecution of the Jews after the murder of von Rath. Not since the world war have we lost so much credit in the world. . . . I am most deeply troubled about the effect on our national life, which is dominated ever more inexorably by a system capable of such things. . . . There is probably nothing more distasteful in life than to have to acknowledge the justice of attacks made by foreigners on one's own people.[18]

Adam arrived home at Imshausen at the end of November resolved to take an active part in the opposition to Hitler. On December 6 he wrote to Sheila Grant Duff:

> I spoke with a cousin in Frankfurt, a friend from Hamburg and an uncle from Berlin. They all think nothing can be done without bowing to the formula. The field after that is wide and full of opportunities but the starting point is evil and closes down the real wells of one's strength or possibilities.[19]

Return to Germany and Resistance

'Bowing to the formula' meant joining the Nazi party. It was necessary to use coded phrases because all letters were censored. The cousin in Frankfurt was Adalbert von Unruh, Professor of Aeronautical Law at the university. The uncle from Berlin was Eberhard von Schweinitz, his mother's youngest brother, who preceded Adam as a Rhodes Scholar at Balliol in 1903–5. The friend from Hamburg was a lawyer, Peter Bielenberg, who had planned to emigrate with his English-born wife Christabel and their sons to Ireland, but was dissuaded from doing so by Adam after visiting him at Imshausen during the Christmas holiday. Christabel Bielenberg has described the situation:

> Adam was now back, Adam had been to Berlin, and the news which Peter brought home after his visit was exhilarating enough and also promising enough to have convinced him that we had been wrong to think of leaving Germany at a moment when the tide was on the turn. At long last the dissident voices of some years back had become a chorus; with a possible world war on their hands, the Generals who commanded the only weapon capable of overthrowing the regime were sufficiently alarmed to be ready to act. More, the nucleus of a civilian government capable of taking over after Hitler's arrest was forming.[20]

Peter Bielenberg subsequently obtained a post in the Reich Ministry of Economics and worked with Adam against the Nazis.

Soon after his return, Adam learned to his surprise and delight that in the previous September, just before the Munich conference, there had been a full scale plot to overthrow Hitler. It was led by General Franz Halder, who had succeeded General Ludwig Beck as Chief of Staff of the German Army in August 1938. The plot centred on the belief that if Britain stood firm over Hitler's claim to the Sudetenland, an invasion of Czechoslovakia would follow. The generals would then arrest Hitler and take over the government in Berlin. When, on September 26, Hitler made a violent speech in which he promised 'The Sudetenland will be my last territorial demand in Europe', General Hans Oster, Deputy Head of Armed Forces Intelligence, informed the conspirators that war against Czechoslovakia was about to be declared. On September 28 the military putsch was set for the next day and at noon General Erwin von Witzleben, the Army Commander, Berlin District, went to General Halder's office to receive orders that would start the putsch. Then came news that Neville Chamberlain and Daladier (French Prime Minister) would meet Hitler in Munich on the following day. General Halder told American Army interrogators after the war that when that news was received, 'I took back the orders, because the entire basis for the action had been taken away'. Halder was further questioned on this point:

> QUESTION: Do I understand you to say that if Mr Chamberlain had not come to Munich, your plan would have been executed, and Hitler would have been deposed?
> HALDER: I can only say the plan would have been executed. I do not know if it would have been successful.[21]

Although details of the plan had been sent to the British Foreign Secretary, Lord Halifax, in advance, the British and French Governments could not be sure that a firm stand at Munich would have brought about a revolt within Germany; and both Prime Ministers knew that their countries were not in a position to go to war. In Britain the Munich agreement was greeted with relief and enthusiasm by the population who realized that Chamberlain had bought valuable time. All that can be said with confidence, in the light of what is now known, is that the chances of an internal revolt against Hitler were greater just before Munich than at any time afterwards until the tide of conquest turned in 1943.

The seniority of the officers involved was impressive and encouraged Adam to think that a coup was possible. They included General Halder, General Beck, General Oster of Armed Forces Intelligence, General von Stulpnagel and General von Witzleben.

The first of his four visits to England in 1939 came in February. It was made on behalf of Ernst von Weizsacher, head of the German Foreign Office, to assess British opinion. He visited Oxford and was surprised and hurt by the coolness with which his friends received him. The Munich agreement of the previous September, although it had saved the peace, seemed to have made people reluctant to have any further dealings with Hitler. Even so, and accepting the changed mood in the country, it was unfortunate to say the least that his Oxford friends could not, or would not, differentiate between Nazis and non-Nazis. For obvious reasons, he could not divulge knowledge of potential plots and coups; all he could indicate was that if peace could be preserved for a little longer, there was a possibility of Hitler being toppled by a military coup inside Germany. When he returned to Germany, he was accompanied by Geoffrey Wilson of the Foreign Office who he had known at Oxford, so that Wilson could see that there was a genuine opposition in Germany and meet some of those involved.

By the summer of 1939 most people in Britain were feeling that war was inevitable and that no diplomacy could stop Hitler's warlike aims.

Return to Germany and Resistance

Adam and his friends, however, were determined to try to avert war, which they believed would be disastrous for Germany and for the whole of Europe. They therefore conceived a new plan and on 1st June he flew to London, hoping to put it before the British Government. His mission, although not initiated by von Weizsacher, the Permanent State Secretary in the German Foreign Office, probably had his approval; and it was certainly cleared with Walter Hewel, Ribbentrop's liaison officer with Hitler. Briefly, the plan was that Hitler should restore freedom to Czechoslovakia and, in return, he should be given Danzig and the Polish Corridor. They suggested that Britain should make this proposal which would return Europe to the pre-Munich position. Hitler would almost certainly soon break the agreement (even if he accepted it) and the German Army would then arrest him and effect a coup. David Astor invited Adam to dinner at Cliveden on the 3rd of June, where he met Lord Halifax, Foreign Secretary, and Lord Lothian. After dinner Adam talked to Halifax, making his point that ordinary Germans, although hurt by the Versailles Treaty twenty years earlier, did not want war. He also told Halifax that the Nazis were planning something with Russia – which transpired to be the German-Soviet Pact of August 1939. Halifax was impressed and said that Chamberlain should hear what he had to say. On June 7 Adam saw Chamberlain at Downing Street. The only other person present was Lord Dunglass (Sir Alec Douglas-Home), Parliamentary Private Secretary to Chamberlain. No official record of the conversation exists and when asked about it a few years ago, Sir Alec could remember nothing of it. Chamberlain and Halifax were impressed by Adam and there is some evidence that a speech made by Halifax at Chatham House on June 29 incorporated some of what Adam had said at Downing Street.

It is important to see the visit to Downing Street in the context of Adam's short life. In ten years he had come a long way from being a theology student at Mansfield and a Rhodes Scholar at Balliol to negotiating with the British Prime Minister in Downing Street. And he was still under thirty years of age.

He returned to Germany on 9th June, but came back to Britain on 11th June; he stayed first with the Astors and then visited Oxford, speaking to friends such as Christopher Hill and Maurice Bowra. He spoke of the need of more talks with Hitler – but he could not tell them that the time gained would be used for a military coup. Friendship turned to suspicion, particularly on the part of Bowra in whom Adam confided that he was working for the opposition in Germany. Notwithstanding that information, Bowra decided that he was playing a double game, refused any further contact with him, and then wrote to Felix

Return to Germany and Resistance

Frankfurter, President Roosevelt's close friend, urging him to treat Adam with the greatest suspicion. Bowra knew that he was planning to visit the United States in the autumn and the letter meant that Adam's US mission was doomed to failure. It seems inconceivable that Bowra, Warden of Wadham College, should make such an assessment, not only without justification, but without any evidence. In his autobiography in 1967, Bowra wrote:

> I decided that von Trott was playing a double game and trying to weaken our resistance just when at last it was beginning to grow stronger. I was wrong. What I overestimated was the competence of the Gestapo, who could be extraordinarily blind and seem actually not to have known about von Trott's efforts against Hitler. So my reason for suspicion was actually quite unfounded. . . . My rejection of him remains one of my bitterest regrets.[22]

The following weekend, June 17–18, he stayed at Sheila Grant Duff's house and at a party met Churchill's daughter Diana and her husband, Duncan Sandys. It was hoped this might lead to a meeting with Churchill, who through the summer had been receiving others involved in the resistance, including General Ewald von Kleist, Count Helmuth James von Moltke and Fabian von Schlabrendorff. However, the attempt to effect a meeting with Churchill was unsuccessful. After the war Churchill told von Schlabrendorff that his staff had consistently misled him about the strength and size of the anti-Hitler movement in Germany during the war.

This was the last time Adam saw Sheila Grant Duff; their friendship was by now overwhelmed by the realities of European politics. In a letter in mid-August 1939 he wrote on brown Chinese paper with a blossoming fruit tree as watermark:

> I hate this constant pathetic leave-taking, but when we are finally cut off, I do not want the smallest drop of bitterness to poison our mutual memory – let's bury the best European friendship deep in the soil, so it cannot be harmed by any winter or surface destruction and may blossom out again like these Chinese ones.[23]

On this visit he also saw his friend Diana Hubback for the last time. In the summer he had written to her:

> Pray that we may keep this peace, precarious as it may be, it is better

Return to Germany and Resistance

than another wholesale return to collective crime. That (peace) is what I am working for now.[24]

In June she was recovering from an operation in the Royal Free Hospital where he visited her. 'I am so tired. There is so much to be done' he told her. In her autobiography she wrote:

> I knew that Adam would continue the struggle in whatever way he could. He wrote guardedly from Basle in 1941, but clearly indicating the course he had set for himself –
>> Recently (he wrote) there have been several indications that you over in your country tend more and more to consider us as being already under the Teuton fold or identified with their aims. Actually this is less and less the case in German Switzerland and you and your friends must insist on this distinction. Personally I have no doubt that you still do.[25]

In March 1942 she received her last letter from him:

> We think and talk of you so often and hope that, in spite of all, there remains at heart a realm of peace in which one day we may meet again.[26]

He flew home on 22 June 1939, but in mid-July he was back in England. As far as is known, he saw only the Astors and Cripps on this visit. He stayed only a few days before returning to Berlin. It was the last time he saw David Astor, although they remained closely in touch. On August 19th Peter Bielenberg flew to London on behalf of Adam in a last-minute attempt to avert war. Through Astor he delivered a message to the British Government urging them to send a military figure such as General Lord Gort, VC direct to Hitler with a letter from the King himself, warning that if Poland was invaded, European war would break out. The idea was that if the proposed visit were made with the utmost publicity, pressure of opinion in Germany might lead the generals to act. The Foreign Secretary would not see Bielenberg and the mission failed. (A similar idea had already been discussed in official circles, the preferred emissary being General Sir Edmund Ironside.)

The Nazi–Soviet Pact was signed on August 23. War seemed inevitable, but still Adam did not give up. Through a friend in the British Embassy he sent a short memorandum on the aims of the German resistance, 'Inner Political Situation in Germany Today', in which he warned that the opposition would be ready to 'use the same methods against

Fascism as Hitler uses now'. He ended, 'If there is a war it is hoped that the inner development of the opposition is strong enough to become really active'.[27]

9
The 3rd of September 1939

There was an eerie stillness in the air in Britain as Sunday, September 3 dawned. It was two days since Hitler had ordered his tanks to cross the Polish border and no-one now believed that he would withdraw back to the frontier. Throughout the land, in homes and factories, people turned on their wireless sets to hear the Prime Minister's speech at 11.15 a.m. It was a broadcast that went down in history:

> I am speaking to you from No. 10 Downing Street. This morning the British ambassador in Berlin handed the German Government a final note, stating that, unless the British Government heard from them by 11 o'clock that they were prepared at once to withdraw their troops from Poland, a state of war would exist between us. I have to tell you now that no such undertaking has been received and that consequently this country is at war with Germany.

Adam von Trott was in the home of his friends Peter and Christabel Bielenberg. She has described the scene very poignantly:

> At war with Germany – at war with Germany – the silence was so deep that the precise voice might have had the sitting room to itself. Adam, who was leaning against the mantelpiece, sighed and turned and glanced at the wireless and Peter and I sat motionless on the sofa, hand in hand. The voice carried on with its message, but I was no longer listening. It was as if each of us was away in separate worlds, groping hesitantly towards just what meaning those words would have for us. The room seemed very small, much too small, and I got up suddenly and went out through the French windows into the garden. Peter made a move to stop me, but he seemed to understand, and sat back again and let me go. The air outside was gentle and warm. A pungent smell of pine trees from the Grunewald hung over the garden and it was very dark.
>
> I sat down on the low brick wall which separated our flower beds

from the lawn, and stared into the darkness. At war with Germany. Through the crack in the sitting room curtains I could see that Adam had moved and was sitting next to Peter on the sofa. They were talking together, leaning forward, staring into the fire, and the flickering flames lit up their faces and threw their dancing shadows on the ceiling. They looked very young, somehow unfairly young to have tried to stem the tide of history.[28]

The next five years were to test Adam's diplomatic skills to the full. As a senior Foreign Office official he was able to travel to neutral countries – he visited Switzerland seven times and Sweden at least four times during 1940 to 1944. In September 1939 he sailed to America to attend a conference of the Institute of Pacific Relations at Virginia Beach. He was representing the Foreign Office, but he tried to use the visit to enlarge and strengthen his contacts on behalf of the opposition. However, he was under suspicion, largely due to the letter Bowra had sent to Felix Frankfurter. President Roosevelt himself treated the matter less seriously, but American officials convinced themselves, and were convinced by Bowra, that Adam was playing a double game. He himself realized this and wrote to David Astor that 'my usefulness over here is very limited'. Astor wrote to him whilst he was in America:

> There are many people here who would wish you to be in this country. What you should do in this matter you can best judge for yourself. I must, however, emphasise that my own feeling is that your usefulness is ten times as great outside Germany as a planner for the future than inside Germany as a revolutionary.[29]

On December 26 he replied, indicating his firm resolve:

> Though I shall listen carefully to the advice you may still send me . . . not to return, I have definitely made up my mind that apart from definite indications of presumable liquidation my place during this coming time is at home. You and your friends may be right that my capacities to do a lot there may be limited, but the urgent need for every single individual with any scope and insight seems to be overwhelmingly on the side of inside work. If this is not recognized by people like ourselves we must resign to an almost helpless determination, because the drift of things, left to themselves, is definitely against what we hope for.[30]

He returned to Germany in January 1940. In his letter of 26 December 1939 he outlined his goal:

We are not fighting within the framework of a constitution on sectional interests and principles, but for the formation of a constitution – which has become an elemental necessity, for the life of Europe as a whole, if our individual countries and what we consider worth preserving in them is to survive. In this sense I think we stand on common ground, not only with responsible conservatives and socialists in our own, but with the analogous alliance in every other country.[31]

From then onwards his close friends in Britain did not know what he was doing, but those who trusted him were confident that he was continuing to work for the downfall of Nazism and the establishment of peace and a new order in Europe. He did, in fact, communicate with A. D. Lindsay in 1942 about the possibility of peace terms.

On 1 June 1940 he joined the Foreign Office. Eight days later, on the 8th of June, he married Clarita Tiefenbacher. In his wedding speech he expressed fears for his friends across the Channel and what they might have to endure in the forthcoming bombing of British cities. His marriage gave him what his cousin described as an 'extremely happy and harmonious union during those vital last years'.

10

The Plea for Recognition

From 1940 onwards Adam did an extensive amount of travelling. As the war progressed, so the number of his visits to neutral and occupied countries increased – from 1940 to July 1944 he went seven times to Switzerland, four times to Sweden, four times to the Low Countries, once to Turkey, and there were probably other visits too.

During the Battle of Britain in September 1940 he visited Geneva to see his old friend W. A. Visser't Hooft, whom he had first met in 1928, and gave him an analysis of the situation in Germany. He told Visser't Hooft that he felt strongly that all those who held the same fundamental Christian convictions about the social and international order were on the same side in the war, even if their governments were on opposite sides.[32] During 1941 and 1942 he went several times to Geneva and his visit in April 1942 was specially important. He heard about Visser't Hooft's plan to visit Britain and this offered Adam an excellent opportunity to contact his friends there. His old friend Sir Stafford Cripps was now in the British Government, so Adam wrote a memorandum to be handed to Sir Stafford. The memorandum, which was naturally unsigned, expressed the thinking of a large part of the opposition in Germany. By now he was much more hopeful about the success of a coup d'état than he had been in 1940 (when Hitler's military successes had somewhat stifled the opposition), but much would depend on the attitude of the Allied governments. The memorandum therefore appealed to the British leaders to take the German opposition seriously; it stated that the most urgent and immediate task was the overthrow of the Hitler regime as soon as possible. They had support from all sections of society and from influential groups in the churches, the military and the public services. They wanted a federal Europe within which all member nations would have the right of self-determination. The memorandum was, in part, a plea for a European Community as it is now developing. Perhaps Adam and his friends were fifty years ahead of their time.

When Visser't Hooft arrived in London in May he handed the memorandum to Sir Stafford Cripps, with copies to Sir Alfred Zimmern, Professor of International Relations at Oxford, and Professor Arnold Toynbee, Director of the Royal Institute of International Affairs, who had been a member of the British delegation at the Versailles Conference in 1919. Cripps took it to Churchill who endorsed it 'very encouraging', but the British Government maintained the position that Germany must be totally defeated militarily and must surrender. Visser't Hooft asked if this was the only answer he could take back to Adam. Sir Stafford replied that it was indeed the only answer, as it was necessary to demonstrate that what the Nazi regime had done could not be tolerated; there would have to be a definite surrender, but the peace would not be a peace of revenge. The Allies would follow a positive policy and seek to establish a new order in Germany. In the meantime the Germans should dissociate themselves from the Nazi regime.

Toynbee handed his copy to Professor Tom Marshall of the Foreign Office Research Unit on Germany, who asked Richard Crossman to comment on it. Crossman, who was working for the German language broadcasts at the BBC, wrote a very personal and supercilious report on May 27:

> I knew Adam von Trott throughout his period at Oxford, a difficult period of transition from democratic to Nazi Germany. A tall, extremely handsome young man, he was probably the most successful German Rhodes Scholar in achieving popularity both among dons and undergraduates. He always claimed to be Hegelian Socialist which meant, in fact, he had vague socialist ideals but came from too good a family to link them with the working class movement in anything but theory. He took his philosophy very seriously indeed; of the quality of that philosophy one can best judge when one remembers that he did not find the Master of Balliol a confused thinker. Indeed I think that the close friendship of the Master of Balliol is due to the fact that in the realm of philosophy each is as high minded as he is woolly. Adam always found me slightly too earthy in my outlook on politics and I always found him so Hegelian that almost any action could be given its dialectical justification however slippery it might have been. In brief, I did not trust him very far, and he did not trust me. In either 1936 or 1937 my wife and I during a tour of Germany stayed at Kassel where Adam was supposed to be training as a lawyer. We saw him every day . . . and my feelings were even more strongly confirmed that in any serious political conflict Adam's high minded idealism would somehow twist to avoid the really unpleasant decision to work for a revolution in Germany.

The Plea for Recognition

The private paper which Visser't Hooft brought from Adam for the personal perusal of Cripps, Temple and Lindsay, is an almost perfect specimen of Adam's thought, ingenuous in its politics and unaware of its intellectual and political dishonesty.

I believe therefore that the group Adam represents really does exist and that it is of some importance for our Political Warfare and it could be misdirected by us in ways useful to HMG. Adam von Trott is not fully aware of his ingenuousness in politics, can claim a really extensive knowledge of England, and may therefore be able to persuade harder headed men than himself to share his illusions.[33]

Cripps asked Eden for the Foreign Office attitude to the memorandum and Geoffrey Harrison minuted on 6 June 1942 that the –

main new point is that the alleged anti-Hitler group is prepared to assassinate Hitler in a coup d'état . . . we can tell Sir S. Cripps that it very probably represents the views of certain elements in Germany in the civil service, army and church. (I am a little doubtful about Labour circles.) On the other hand we do not think the time has yet come for us to intervene directly to encourage this group and we should see active signs of its existence before we should believe it was of real significance.[34]

On June 12 Harrison wrote another minute:

I think I should draw attention to the fact that it is really very dangerous for documents of the nature of this memorandum to be circulating in this country . . . it can only be embarrassing if influential people are stimulated in this way to interfere in both our policy and political warfare towards Germany. Moreover, Visser't Hooft has moved freely in various circles in this country . . . it is therefore for consideration whether, as we cannot expect to control visitors of this kind, we should deny them entry at all in future into this country.

He also referred to Cripps's suggestion that Miss Elizabeth Wiskemann (a friend and contact of Adam in the British Legation in Berne) should be more careful about her contact with Adam because of his value as an opponent of Hitler:

I understand that Sir S. Cripps suggested that Miss Wiskeyman (sic) should be told to 'cool off' Adam von Trott on the grounds that he is too valuable. It seems to me regrettable that it should be known that Herr von Trott is in contact at all with Miss Wiskeyman (sic) and I am very doubtful about asking her to 'cool him off'. In fact I do not think it is in our interest to do so since his value to us as a 'martyr' is likely to exceed his value to us in post-war Germany.[35]

In a minute on the 8th of June, Harrison had written:

The indications are that these individuals are in fact less concerned with active steps in eliminating the Nazis than in stepping into the Nazis' shoes when the Nazis have been eliminated.[36]

The Foreign Office accepted Crossman's briefing, ignoring Cripps and Adam's other distinguished friends.

Soon after Visser't Hooft returned to Geneva, Adam visited him again. In his memoirs Visser't Hooft described the scene:

When I told him about the British reaction to his memorandum he was so deeply disappointed that he was near despair. What I could tell him about the good intentions of the British was no consolation. He felt that the men whom he considered as comrades-in-arms in the battle against Hitler had let him down. The supra-national solidarity of men defending the same fundamental values on which he had counted so strongly had been denied. That was a terribly hard thing to accept. And there would now be much less chance of creating a really effective opposition in Germany. Adam felt obviously that he had failed in the very mission with which he had been entrusted. It was no wonder that there was bitterness in his words. We sat for a long time in my garden on that warm summer night. I tried to find words to encourage him, but all I could do was to show that I understood what this blow meant to him.[37]

At the same time as Visser't Hooft was in London, Dr George Bell, Bishop of Chichester, was visiting Stockholm. Adam had learned of his visit from Visser't Hooft and arranged for two German pastors, Hans Schoenfeld and Dietrich Bonhoeffer, to visit Stockholm to meet Bell and give him details of the opposition and of the planned coup d'état, together with a copy of the memorandum that Visser't Hooft had taken to London. Bonhoeffer, who before the war had been pastor of two German churches in London, had known Bell for nine years. He now gave Bell the names of the chief conspirators, including Beck, von Hammerstein,

Goerdler, Leuschner, Kaiser, Schacht, Prince Louis Ferdinand, von Kluge and von Witzleben. He asked for an assurance that, once the whole Hitler regime had been overthrown, the Allied Governments would treat with a bona fide German Government for a peace settlement which would include withdrawal of all German forces from occupied countries and reparation for damages; and he requested that the assurance should either be given to an authorized representative of the opposition or announced publicly. If the former was the preferred method, it was proposed that the ideal intermediary to receive the assurance was Adam von Trott. Bell discussed all this with Sir Victor Mallett, the British ambassador, who reported to the Foreign Office that this was 'something more than one of the usual peace feelers'.

When Bell returned he saw Eden, the Foreign Secretary, at the end of June and asked for some encouragement to be given to the German opposition movement. Eden confirmed that some of the names given by Bonhoeffer were already known by the Foreign Office, which had been informed by other sources of the existence of the plot; however, such information was not taken seriously, nor was it wished to encourage anti-Nazis in their aims to overthrow Hitler. On July 17 Eden wrote to Bell that he was 'satisfied that it would not be in the national interest for any reply whatever to be sent'.

11
The Kreisau Circle

The group which from 1941 onwards provided the spiritual and political ideology behind attempts to overthrow Hitler was the Kreisau Circle. It took its name from the estate of Count Helmuth James von Moltke at Kreisau in Upper Silesia, where the group sometimes met.

Von Moltke, whose maternal grandfather was Chief Justice of the Transvaal and whose great, great uncle was Field Marshal von Moltke of Bismarck's wars, maintained close contacts with England and, after the Nazis came to power, prepared to be called to the English bar. When war broke out in 1939 he was attached to the Supreme Command of the German Armed Forces as adviser on law and economic affairs. He and Count Peter Yorck von Wartenberg shared the view that it was important to prepare for the spiritual and physical rehabilitation of Germany after its inevitable defeat and they gathered a group around them for this purpose. By 1943 there were over twenty men representing the churches, the outlawed Social Democratic party, academics, lawyers, businessmen, economists, trade unionists and diplomats. After von Moltke and Yorck von Wartenberg, the most influential of the group was Adam von Trott, whose task was to advise the members of the group on foreign policy and to represent the views of the group to the Allied governments through his extensive contacts.

The group's first main meeting was at Whitsun 1942. There were two later meetings at Kreisau in October 1942 and Whitsun 1943, but there were frequent more informal discussions at von Moltke's house in Berlin, Peter Yorck's home in the Berlin suburb of Lichterfelde, and Adam von Trott's flat at Dahlem. The members of the group, mostly of the younger generation, differed from many of the older opponents of the Nazis, e.g. the generals of the 1938 plot, in that many of the latter sought a return to a pre-Weimar Germany, whereas the Kreisau group looked towards a new Germany which would be an equal partner in a new Europe. This fitted in completely with Adam's view that family wars (as he called them) would only be ended when there was a European solution. In a letter to

The Kreisau Circle

Lionel Curtis on 18 April 1942, von Moltke summed up the younger men's view of the new Europe which they hoped would follow the elimination of Hitler:

> For us Europe after the war is less a problem of frontiers and soldiers, of top heavy organizations or grand plans; Europe after the war is more a question of how the picture of man can be re-established in the breasts of our fellow-citizens. This is a question of religion and education, of ties of work and family, of the proper relation of responsibility and rights. . . . Please do not forget, that we trust that you will stand it through without flinching as we are prepared to do our bit, and don't forget that for us a very bitter end is in sight when you have seen matters through. We hope that you will realize that we are ready to help you to win war and peace.[38]

The Kreisau Circle was penetrated at a tea party in Berlin in September 1943, given by Frau Hannah Solf, widow of the last Imperial German Foreign Minister. She and Elizabeth von Thadden, the headmistress of a well-known school for girls, were at the centre of a small circle of anti-Nazi intellectuals. A Gestapo spy infiltrated the group and was at the tea party when people spoke freely of their hatred of the regime. Consequently all their telephones were then tapped. As a result the whole of the tea party group, plus some others, were arrested, including Fraulein von Thadden, Frau Solf and her daughter, Countess Ballestrem, Hilger von Scherpenberg (Schacht's son-in-law), Otto Kiep (former Consul in New York), Kunzer of the Foreign Office, and Albrecht von Bernstorff, who was Adam's old friend. In mid-January 1944 von Moltke was arrested. All were executed except the Solfs, who miraculously survived because of Japanese intervention (her husband had been ambassador in Japan and was popular there).

The arrest of von Moltke broke up the Kreisau Circle. The attack on Hitler on July 20 came as a surprise to him, as he had been in prison since January. He was not himself in favour of assassination, preferring to plan for the future and await the inevitable military defeat. On the 10th and 11th of January 1945, after a year in prison, he was tried and sentenced to death; the sentence was carried out on the 23rd. In a farewell letter written to his wife on 10th and 11th of January he mentioned his friend Adam:

> All the pains God has taken with me, the intricate twists and turns of conduct, the infinite detours, the purport of it all was suddenly revealed

within an hour on January 10th, 1945. All that seemed obscure at long last gains a meaning: Mami and Papi, the brothers and sister, the little sons, Kreisau and its needs, the labour camps, my hatred of flag-waving and refusal to join the Party or any of its offshoots, Curtis and the journeys to England, Adam and Peter and Carlo, all that became intelligible at last, within the span of one brief hour. And to think that God gave himself so much trouble, just for that one hour![39]

12

Fanning the Flames of Resistance

In January 1943 Adam contacted Allen Dulles who had been sent to Berne as head of the US Office of Strategic Services; his special task was to keep in touch with anti-Nazis. Adam expressed his belief that, with the rejection of his overtures by the British government, the conspirators might be tempted to turn to the Russians for help in overthrowing Hitler. Washington reported this to London, but no action was taken on it.

His next visit was to Istanbul in June 1943 where he told the German ambassador, Franz von Papen, of the plot. The ambassador was generally in sympathy, but nothing came of the meeting. Von Papen, known as 'the fox', was a former Chancellor of Germany who was noted for his ability to extricate himself from any difficult situation. At first he opposed Hitler, then he served him. He was one of those tried at Nuremberg after the war; he was one of the three who were acquitted.

On 27 October 1943 Adam went to Stockholm for six days and met two attachés from the British Legation. He outlined Operation Valkyrie, the plan that was put into operation the following July, and asked if, once a revolution had taken place, the unconditional surrender formula would be given up and heavy bombing suspended. After the war one of the attachés, Roger Hinks, wrote of Adam:

> I met one of the most charming, honest and decent men I have ever had the pleasure of meeting.[40]

The words 'unconditional surrender' were first used at the final press conference at the Casablanca Anglo-American Conference on 24 January 1943, when President Roosevelt announced:

> Peace can only come by the total elimination of German and Japanese

Fanning the Flames of Resistance

war power . . . elimination of German, Japanese and Italian war power means unconditional surrender by Germany, Italy and Japan.

There has always been some division of opinion as to whether or not the policy of unconditional surrender had been definitely agreed between Churchill and Roosevelt. When the proposed joint statement to be issued at the end of the conference was being discussed, Churchill referred it to the War Cabinet who agreed with his view that Italy should be excluded, in the hope that this would encourage a break-up of the Italian Government. Churchill thought this had been accepted by Roosevelt and, as he wrote after the war, 'It was with some feeling of surprise that I heard the President say at the Press Conference on January 24 that we would enforce unconditional surrender upon all our enemies. General Ismay, who was also present at all discussions of the Chiefs of Staff when the communiqué was prepared, was also surprised'. In the official joint statement prepared by the Chiefs of Staff, approved by Churchill and Roosevelt, and then approved by the War Cabinet, there was no mention of unconditional surrender. Churchill later acknowledged that there had probably been a misunderstanding between them about what they had agreed. Roosevelt himself wrote that 'suddenly the Press Conference was on, and Winston and I had had no time to prepare for it, and the thought popped into my mind that they had called Grant (in the American Civil War) "Old Unconditional Surrender", and the next thing I knew I had said it.'[41]

The reasoning behind the policy was sound because there was general acceptance in Britain and America that this time Germany must be completely defeated so that there could be no repetition of the 1918 claim of the military being stabbed in the back by the politicians. The slogan was also thought likely to appeal to Stalin as proof that the West would not come to terms with a non-communist Germany at his expense. It also fitted in with the British Government's policy of 'absolute silence' towards peace moves which was first promulgated at the end of December 1940 after peace enquiries had come from a Swedish citizen in Berne on behalf of Goering. A year earlier, in December 1939, Halifax had authorized Captain Payne Best, a secret service agent, to meet German representatives at Venlo near the Dutch frontier with Germany. Best and his companions were abducted and taken to Germany. Payne Best spent the remainder of the war in prison and on 24 February 1945 was taken to Buchenwald, where his cell was directly opposite that of Dietrich Bonhoeffer. On Easter Day, 1 April, they left Buchenwald, where they could hear the American guns. A few days later they arrived at Schonberg, where they were housed in a school. On the following Sunday Bonhoeffer was told to get ready to leave. He knew what it meant and said his farewells to his fellow prisoners for whom he had just conducted a morning service at their request. He asked Payne Best, if he survived, to contact the Bishop of Chichester, Dr Bell, to convey his greetings to his old friend and to tell him that 'for me it is the end but also the beginning'. Bonhoeffer was taken to Flossenburg where he was hanged in the early hours of Monday morning, 9 April.

It was with the Venlo incident in mind that at the end of December 1940 Churchill minuted to Anthony Eden, Foreign Secretary:

> Your predecessor was entirely misled in December 1939. Our attitude towards all such enquiries should be absolute silence.[42]

The impact of the words 'unconditional surrender' gave Goebbels an opportunity he did not miss. He used his propaganda machine to the full in convincing the German people that the Allied intention was to destroy Germany completely and crush its people into dust; therefore they must increase their efforts and continue the war – better the privations they were suffering now than the horrors that would come from defeat. For Adam and his friends in the resistance the task had been made much more difficult.

From 18 to 20 December 1943 Adam was in Geneva where he met Robert Elliot of the SCM and Allen Dulles. When he was not making visits to neutral countries he was conducting a hectic round of meetings with other members of the resistance. During 1943 he saw von Hassell, General Karl von Stulpnagel (Military governor of Paris), Count von Moltke, Count Yorck von Wartenburg, Carl Langbehn and Johannes Popitz. In early August he travelled to Belgium to see General von Falkenhausen (Commander in Belgium and Northern France). However, during 1943 the ranks of the resisters were very much depleted, in particular by the arrest of some of the principal members. In April Hans von Dohnanyi, Dietrich Bonhoeffer and Josef Muller were arrested. In the same month General Oster, deputy to Admiral Canaris (head of the Abwehr, the Counter-Intelligence Department of the Military High Command) was suspended from duty and retired. The penetration and arrest of the Solf Circle further depleted the ranks.

As 1943 came to a close it was clear beyond doubt that the tide had turned in the Allies' favour. Italy had surrendered, although a puppet Mussolini 'government' still existed; the British and American forces were poised to complete the liberation of Italy itself; Africa was completely clear of Axis troops; General Eisenhower and his team were planning the Second Front which was to open in the following year. Most German commanders in the field knew that they would not be able to hold their lines against the onslaught that was to come. The German air force no longer posed a threat to the British mainland. And in Germany itself those who despised the Nazi regime and everything it stood for were preparing to take the final gamble to rid their country of the men who were bringing it to ruin.

13
The Year 1944

Adam was always noted for his kindness and it was a kindly act for a friend that put him in great danger early in 1944.

During his visit to Istanbul in June 1943 he had been asked by the head of the Abwehr (the Counter Intelligence Service) there, Professor Paul Leverkuhn, to try to have one of his friends, Erich Vermehren (another resister), transferred from his post at Abwehr headquarters in Berlin to Istanbul. Adam had met Vermehren in 1937 when he was short-listed for a Rhodes Scholarship and Adam was a member of the German Rhodes Scholarship Selection Committee. On his return to Berlin Adam, who as a Legationssekretar (Second Secretary) had the necessary seniority, arranged for Vermehren to be issued with a visa and to be transferred to Istanbul. In the following December Vermehren was on leave in Berlin and asked Adam to arrange for his wife to join him in Istanbul. Adam discussed it with the Foreign Office Personnel Department through Marschall von Bieberstein and the necessary documentation was issued.

The Vermehrens were friends of Otto Kiep, one of those arrested in January 1944 after they had been betrayed after a tea party at Frau Solf's home. Kiep had nominated Vermehren for his Rhodes Scholarship and his arrest naturally caused them alarm. When, shortly afterwards, they were recalled to Berlin, they immediately contacted the British Secret Service in Turkey and defected to the British. They were brought to England and their defection was prominently featured in the British press. On Saturday, 4 March 1944 *The Times* published an article entitled 'A German and his Conscience'. It quoted Vermehren as having given information to the British Intelligence Service, explaining that he was happy to be able to do something for Germany and to join the ranks of those who had declared war against 'the bitterest enemies of Germany – the National Socialists'. He referred to the 'unscrupulous party clique ruining the country'. At a time when Adam was so busily involved in talks in Sweden and Switzerland, shocks such as this must have been very wounding.

1 Adam vot Trott in 1932.

2 Count Helmuth James von Moltke, leader of the Kreisau Circle, on trial in the People's Court, January 1945.

3 General Ludwig Beck, Chief of Army General Staff, 1935–38. He became leader of resistance in the Armed Forces. He was designated Head of State if the 1944 plot had been successful.

4 Colonel Claus Schenk Graf von Stauffenberg (extreme left) standing to attention next to General Friedrich Fromm who is being greeted on arrival at the Wolfsschanze (Wolf's Lair) on 15 July 1944. On Hitler's left, holding a folder, is Field Marshal Wilhelm Keitel, Head of Overall High Command of the Armed Forces.

5 The conference room at the Wolfsschanze after the assassination attempt, 20 July 1944.

6 Adam von Trott, about 1935.

7 Adam's mother, Eleonore von Trott zu Solz (born von Schweinitz).

8 Adam von Trott as a young student.

9 Adam with his father.

10 Adam in Oxford.

11 Adam von Trott, about 1935.

12 Adam von Trott at Cliveden with David Astor.

13 Adam at a conference of the Institute of Pacific Relations, November 1939 (front row, 2nd from right).

14 In Davos, March 1942.

15 Adam during a wartime visit to Basle, autumn 1943.

16 Johannes Winkelmann, Adam von Trott, Peter Bielenberg, summer 1939.

17 Family group at Imshausen, 1944.

18 Hans-Bernd von Haeften on trial in the People's Court. Adam in background.

19 & 20 Adam in the People's Court, 15 August 1944.

21 Memorial stone for Adam von Trott zu Solz and his friends, overlooking Imshausen. The inscription reads – Adam von Trott zu Solz 9.8.1909–26.8.1944. Executed with his friends in the struggle against the destroyers of our homeland. Pray for them. Heed their example.

22 Adam on trial in the *Volksgerichtshof* (People's Court), 15 August 1944.

23 Memorial cross, visible for many miles, on the hill above Imshausen.

24 With Foreign Office colleagues Alexander Worth, Hans Felix Richter, Josias von Rantzau.

25 Wilfrid Israel, Anglo-German, general manager of family department store in Berlin. He travelled freely on his British passport and was able to get many Jews out of Germany. Close friend of Adam.

26 The Rt. Revd. G.K.A. Bell, Bishop of Chichester, close friend of Dietrich Bonhoeffer.

27 With Foreign Office colleagues Hans Felix Richter, Trump, Alexander Worth, Leipholdt.

28 In the uniform of his student corps at Göttingen University.

29 Colonel Claus Schenk Graf von Stauffenberg, who planted the bomb in the conference room at the Wolfsschanze, 20 July 1944.

30 Major-General Henning von Tresckow, leader of resistance on the Eastern front; photograph taken a few days before he took his own life on 21 July 1944. He planted a bomb on Hitler's aeroplane in 1943, but it failed to explode.

31 General Franz Halder, Chief of Army General Staff, 1938–42, leader of the planned Army coup in September 1938.

32 The Revd. Dr W.B. Selbie, Principal of Mansfield College, who brought Adam to Oxford in 1929.

33 Dr Carl Goerdler, former Mayor of Leipzig. He was to become Chancellor-Elect if the 1944 coup had been successful.

34 Dietrich Bonhoeffer, Evangelical pastor and theologian, university chaplain in Berlin, pastoral posts in Spain and London. Worked closely with the Abwehr and resistance groups.

35 Adam and Clarita von Trott.

36 Otto John (with his brother Hans on right). Lawyer at Lufthansa and linked to the Foreign Office resistance group.

37 Field Marshal Erwin von Witzleben who would have seized Government offices and arrested Hitler if the planned 1938 coup had been successful. Later designated to be Commander-in-Chief of the Army if the 1944 plot had been successful.

38 Ulrich von Hassell in the People's Court. Former ambassador in Rome. Key member of Beck–Goerdler section of resistance.

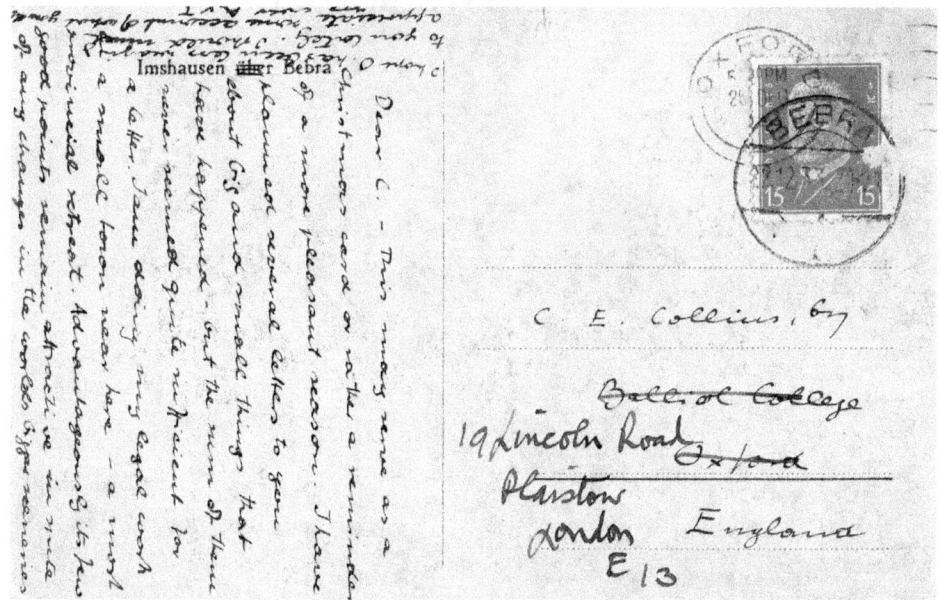

39 Postcard sent to Charles Collins by Adam von Trott at Christmas 1933, eleven months after the Nazis came to power, in which he refers to "changes in the world's bigger scenarios".

40 Imshausen, the von Trott family home.

41 Adam von Trott with Charles Collins and an estate forester at Imshausen, 1932.

It was easy for the Gestapo to trace back the connection between the Vermehren postings to Istanbul and Adam. He was now questioned several times by the Gestapo, but by keeping his nerve and using his outstanding diplomatic skills, he was able to convince them of his innocence. It certainly made him more cautious, especially as at the same time the BBC programmes referred to 'a Rhodes Scholar with peace proposals' during his last visit to Stockholm in October 1943. As his wife Clarita later said, it was a miraculous escape.

Roger Hinks of the British Legation in Stockholm then sent a message saying they would like a further talk with Adam, who decided to take the risk and go. All neutral capitals were hotbeds of agents, British, American and German; and when Adam was walking the streets of those cities, he never knew when he was being trailed by the Gestapo. On this occasion, in March 1944, he decided that the possibility of starting negotiations was so important that it was worth taking the risk. When he arrived he found the British Foreign Office had only wanted to interview him in order to get information about conditions in Germany. In fact, Ewan Butler, a Secret Service agent, recorded that when Legation staff asked permission from London to meet him, it was refused on grounds that the policy was 'unconditional surrender' and there must be no contact with anti-Nazis who wished to dispose of Hitler. After the war Butler wrote, 'The Allies, I am still convinced, missed a great opportunity'.[43]

Whilst in Stockholm he had two talks with a pro-British Swedish friend, Frau Almstrom. These talks were at the request of the British Legation, who asked Frau Almstrom to produce a memorandum on Adam's views. This was forwarded to London. Amongst other things he said that:

> American bombing in daylight of industrial targets was understood by the German people to be a 'necessity', but the relentless British bombing by night with the object of total obliteration of German cities did the British cause much harm.
>
> The Allied terms for an armistice should be constantly broadcast to the German people so that Goebbels would not be able to keep the terms from the German people. If the Allies would communicate what the peace terms would be, he would disclose the names of the generals who were willing to attempt a coup to overthrow Hitler. He recognized the need for a total occupation of Germany and urged that it should be a joint Anglo-Russian-American occupation.
>
> If the generals knew the terms they would, if necessary, make the

The Year 1944

forthcoming Second Front a walkover for the Allies and he had spoken to the generals about 'this very thing'.

The opposition was well organized, but had to keep low as it had no support from outside; he himself could get permission to come to Sweden at any time because he was being treated by a Swedish doctor for a liver complaint. The military must be used, at any rate in the early stages, if the whole of Europe was not to fall into a state of chaos from which it might never recover, as they were the only opposition with sufficient strength to bring about a successful coup.[44]

Finally, Adam gave Frau Almstrom details of life in Berlin. He said that, as a high official, he could travel to work in his own car, but others such as clerks and typists often arrived two hours late. Berlin was a very dreary and empty city and transport problems were acute.

In the same month, March, Adam saw Christabel Bielenberg for the last time. She was passing through Berlin and called unexpectedly at his flat. She was admitted by his maid, Emma, who said he had gone for a walk. Whilst waiting for him to return, she opened the gramophone and saw he had been playing Mozart's Requiem in D Minor. Then she opened a book lying on the table, 'The Last Enemy' by Richard Hillary, a Battle of Britain pilot. Adam then returned and they had lunch together. Christabel Bielenberg has movingly described their conversation in detail. She was talking, but –

Adam did not appear to be listening.

'Yes, I owe more to Oxford than I can say, but it's a strange thing. When I decided to come back to Germany in 1933, I would have thought that I did exactly what most of my Oxford friends would have done, if they had been faced with a Hitler in their country. Yet the very fact that I did come back, when I suppose I could have stayed away, aroused, I think, nothing but distrust – damaging distrust. I sometimes wonder how many friends I have there now – I mean real friends.'

'Now look, Adam,' I said, 'I don't know about your friends, but one thing is certain. You are having to live, yes live, what they, at most, can talk about. There's a big difference.'

Adam pushed back his chair and started pacing the room. 'I don't regret for one single moment that I came back,' he said. 'This is my home, this is where I have my roots, and I am firmly convinced that any German who wants to help in the reconstruction of a post-war Europe must have experienced – personally, intimately what has gone on here in our country. What made a man a Nazi, what makes men sit tight and do nothing, what it has meant to be in opposition, to oppose, always to oppose. The bust-up hopes, the heroism, and there has been heroism, seemingly useless heroism and then the shame – the paralyzing shame. There are things which will need all our strength to unravel – to try to make intelligible after this war is over. Those who left Germany, and may come back afterwards, will be uprooted strangers speaking a different language, and whatever advice they may have to offer, will hardly lure any old dog out from behind the stove.

I can't believe that they want to create a vacuum here in the centre of Europe – a vacuum fills, and if this bombing goes on, it will fill from the East. Even Stalin has realized that when the Nazis are gone he will have to deal with the German people – even he is making overtures. But the Allies, unconditional surrender, unconditional surrender, like a broken gramophone record, we have to face it, I have to face it, that it is the only echo which has come back from across our borders from the West. And yet I know there are people out there who must realize that the Nazis and all they stand for are as much our enemies as theirs.'

I sighed. I wished that I could find some explanation, some answer to the conundrum. Why the distrust? To me, Adam's path had always been crystal clear. . . . It was incomprehensible to me that the British, that the Americans, had not been able to see that they had nothing to lose, and perhaps months of warfare and thousands of lives to save, by encouraging an opposition to Hitler within Germany. Adam had ceased pacing the room and had come to stop by the window. Leaning against the curtain, he was looking out with half-closed eyes over the misty trees, which as yet showed little sign of the coming spring. Behind his head was an engraving of one of his American ancestors, and I was suddenly struck by the physical resemblance between that American statesman and Supreme Court judge and his German great-great-grandson.

'You haven't sent John Jay to the country, I see,' I remarked rather irrelevantly.

'John Jay sticks around with me,' he answered without turning his head, and then, 'my secretary was killed out there the other day. Do you remember Fraulein Walter? A nice, harmless, very loyal little person. Buried under the rubble of her block of flats, with her mother. We tried our best for hours, but we couldn't get near enough for the heat. It's not always easy to confine one's indignation to the circumstances which bring such things about. I wonder why it was that just she had to pay the price. You see how it is, just why we have to plan ahead, to plan for what will come afterwards. It helps us to keep things in proportion. Nothing can really be solved though, there can be no new start until the guns are silent, and we meet with the Allies, around a table, here in Berlin.'

I sighed again. 'Will this war ever end, Adam? Do you believe the Allies will really land in France?'

'Oh yes, they intend to land, they must land sometime. No-one knows exactly when.'

Adam came back across the room and stood in front of me. Somehow his mood seemed to have changed, and something of the old enthusiasm had come back into his voice. 'But perhaps you won't have to wait that long, Chris, not even for the landing, I mean. I don't think that I will be able to go abroad again. The last time I was in Sweden – well, it has become increasingly difficult and dangerous, I guess. I don't know if I could have done more to try and persuade outsiders that there is another Germany, but one way or another I feel that chapter is now closed. I wish I could tell you more, but it's no use burdening you – you'll hear soon enough. We've not been idle, in fact the last weeks, in spite of all, have been positive ones – exciting, in fact. From now on this is a German affair. We must rid ourselves of this regime by ourselves, and believe me if you believe nothing else, it will be done. It will and must be done, before the Allies have to do it for us.'

Adam fetched his bicycle out of the cellar and came along with me to the Falkenried. He had to go to meet someone, he said, and he wanted to be home again before a possible raid because Emma was scared on her own. He had told me just beforehand, with obvious pleasure, that he had had a message from the Rhodes Trust just after Christmas, asking after his welfare. So that was the only official recognition he had been able to gather in, after risking his life again and again bearing testimony to 'another Germany'. Before pedalling away round the corner he turned and gave me a cheery wave and cocked a discreet snook in the direction of the house of the Nazi professor across the road.[45]

By the 1st of April he was back in Berlin, where he entertained Peter Bielenberg, Herbert Blankenhorn and a soldier friend of his younger brother, Heinrich von Trott, to dinner. Afterwards Adam and Blankenhorn took a walk in the nearby Grunewald and later that evening Adam wrote to his wife that Blankenhorn was 'besides Haeften the most capable and sympathetic of the younger colleagues I have found in the office'. Herbert Blankenhorn was a Foreign office official who was in charge of protocol and the re-locating of foreign missions. Adam's high opinion of him was shared by Missie Vassiltchikov who worked as a secretary in Adam's office. On January 28 she recorded in her diary:

> I met Dr Blankenhorn at last under the lantern of a local inn. It was pouring with rain. We climbed a steep hill to his house and settled down for a long chat in the parlour with a bottle of wine and some chocolates. He strikes me as an extremely quick-witted Rhinelander. To say that he foresees the collapse of Germany is putting things mildly. He seems actually to look forward to it and has very definite ideas about Germany's post-defeat future – partition of the country, the creation of individual autonomous Lander, etc![46]

After the war Blankenhorn was able to put his constitutional ideas into practice as one of Chancellor Adenauer's closest advisers and General Secretary of the Christian Democratic Union (CDU).

Adam now returned to Switzerland where he saw Allen Dulles, who had recently talked with Goerdler in Geneva. Dulles had sent a summary of these talks to Washington and later, on May 16, said that he was 'convinced of the sincerity of the emissaries' and asked what the Allied policy was towards the resistance movement and what offers of help they might give. The State Department sent a note to the British ambassador about the talks, but unfortunately omitted to say that Dulles was convinced of the sincerity of the emissaries, i.e. Goerdler and Adam von Trott. On May 24 the British Embassy in Washington transmitted a note to the Foreign Office about the talks in Switzerland, stating that the emissaries claimed to represent a group including Leuschner, a Socialist leader and former Minister of the Interior in Hesse; General Hans Oster (who had been involved in the abortive plot in September 1938), formerly deputy to Admiral Canaris, head of the Abwehr; Carl Goerdler, former Lord Mayor of Leipzig; General Ludwig Beck, former Chief of Staff of the Army; General Franz Halder, former Chief of Staff of the Army (leader of the September 1938 plot); General Kurt Zeitzler, Chief of Staff of the Army since 1942; General Adolf Heusinger, Chief of Operations for the Army under Zeitzler; General Friedrich Olbricht, former Chief of Staff of the Army and, since 1943, deputy commander of the Reserve Army; General Alexander von Falkenhausen, military commander in Belgium and northern France; Field Marshal Gerd von Rundstedt, commander in chief of Army West in France. Although von Rundstedt was mentioned, he was not in fact a member of the group planning the coup. As early as 1942 he knew about the resistance movement among high-ranking officers but, although he was never a convinced Nazi, he refused to commit himself to the conspiracy. He informed Field Marshal Rommel, 'You are young and you are popular with the people. You must do it.' That was as far as he went and he did not betray the plans or those he knew to be involved. After the unsuccessful plot, however, he followed his oath of allegiance to Hitler and presided over the military court of honour that found the military conspirators guilty and expelled them from the armed forces prior to their appearance before the Volksgericht (the People's Court). By expelling them, it meant that they were hanged instead of being shot. Von Rundstedt survived the war. As one of the old-style professional soldiers, he found his conscience troubled on the subject of breaking his oath. He died in Hanover in 1953.

It might have been thought that the naming of so many prominent officers and civilians would have led the Foreign Office to consider very seriously the information from Adam and Goerdler about plans to overthrow the Nazi regime, but it was not so. Sir Alexander Cadogan, Permanent Under Secretary, replied on June 8:

> Please thank State Department for this information and say, 'We fully agree with them in regarding this approach with profound suspicion.'

Geoffrey Harrison, First Secretary (after the war to be British ambassador to Brazil, Persia and the USSR) minuted: 'This looks very bogus.' Frank Roberts (after the war to be British ambassador to Yugoslavia, the USSR and the Federal Republic of Germany) minuted: 'Very bogus and old friends.' P. H. Loxley, private secretary to Cadogan, added: 'Uncle Tom Cobley and all.'[47]

During this visit to Switzerland in April 1944, Adam saw Elizabeth Wiskemann of the British Legation on the 14th; it was to be their last meeting. She later recorded:

> He looked a shadow of his former self, grey and haggard. He was obsessed with the effects of the air raids on Berlin and other German towns, and he brought me photographs of rows of corpses, many those of children. It was a fearful evening. I had to say, 'Adam, this human misery is horrible, but there is no message I could send that would affect the directives given to the RAF; I have nothing whatever to do with the fighting forces directly or indirectly. If I were to say what I think, that this kind of bombing is bad policy as well as cruel, it would make no difference . . . ' He was like a broken man and said he expected to be arrested soon after his return to Germany. The usual exchange follows: 'Must you go back?' 'Yes, I absolutely must.' After he had left

he telephoned me once more. . . . I forget what he had to say, but I told him that he had left his gloves behind, a very fine pair. He said, 'Keep them as a gage'. For his safety, he meant – I think I had the sense not to say any more.[48]

On his return from the April visit to Switzerland, Adam continued with his plans and meetings. A series of bombing raids had destroyed the offices in which he worked and he and his colleagues were now in cramped conditions in the Karlsbader Hotel. Missie Vassiltchikov saw him on his trips from the Sudeten Mountains, where her office had been transferred. On the the 1st of May he and Colonel Claus Schenk Graf von Stauffenberg had dinner alone together in Adam's Dahlem flat. Beforehand Adam had written to his wife, 'Emma is in the kitchen preparing dinner for myself and a good friend.' On the following evening Missie saw him; the entry in her diary for that day starts with a somewhat delightful example of the entrepreneurial spirit in war-torn Berlin and then refers to her meeting with Adam:

> This morning I managed to exchange Percy Frey's meat coupons, which had expired, against a big sausage. Then, at the office, I staged a small auction and a girl bought it off me for a little less than it was worth, but paying for it in valid coupons, which I will now return to Percy. I am very proud!
> Stayed at the office until late; then drove with Adam Trott back to his home and had supper with him there. He is a man completely out of the ordinary. All his thoughts and efforts focus on things and values of a higher order, to which neither the mood of this country, nor that of the Allies seem attuned. He belongs to a more civilized world – something, alas, neither side does.[49]

Since the invasion of Italy by the Allies, the German embassy in Italy had been located on Lake Garda and Adam's old friend, Albrecht von Kessel, was based there. Shortly before Whitsun Adam, who had been promoted to the rank of Counsellor in April, and his friend spent a few days in Venice. Here, in a city he had not previously visited, he was able to relax; and although all the museums were closed, he found a peace of mind in an atmosphere that suited him intellectually. They then went on to Verona. When they said goodbye at Verona station, Adam said, 'At least we know that one of us is safe'. During their short holiday, von Kessel asked him to organize a posting for himself to Rome, suggesting that he might be risking his life in a lost cause. Adam replied that it might

The Year 1944

be too late, but the attempt must be made; German honour would never recover unless it could be said that there were Germans who had the courage and the determination to rise against their oppressors.

Whitsun fell at the end of May and Adam took the opportunity to visit his family at Imshausen. It was the last time he was to be in his home which had always meant so much to him. It was also the last time he saw his mother, his sister Vera and his two little girls, Verena and Clarita. In her memoir on his life, his wife said that it was as if he knew that this was the last time:

> In the glow of a warm and bright early summer's day we went for a last walk over the hills, and while we were on the hilltops he took in scene after scene of his beloved homeland. On the way back he told me that in Berlin, where he was returning, these scenes would remain in his mind's eye and give him strength. He told me also that he thought calmly about his own fate. If he was needed, God would preserve his life, and if not, he accepted his fate with resignation. His simple words, and the way that, quite contrary to his usual custom, he spoke directly of God and the last things, filled me with joy and fear at the same time. His expression was one of complete harmony and its beauty was moving. His mother told me afterwards that she had had the same impression. During the war I sometimes seemed to notice such changes of expression in young soldiers, shortly before they met death.[50]

Reports that plans were afoot to assassinate Hitler and overthrow the Nazi regime were circulating among the German military through 1943 and the first half of 1944. Tatiana Vassiltchikov, a sister of Missie, had married Prince Paul Metternich, who was serving with the Spanish Division with the German army in Russia. In her country home at Konigswart on an autumn day in 1943, she was visited by Missie. 'They are planning a coup d'etat against Hitler', Missie told her. 'It is apparently important for them to know the mood of the higher échelons of the Army should it take place. To sound this out, the conspirators are moving staff officers they can trust into key positions. There are rumours that Paul's name has been mentioned, and that he is going to be approached. If things go wrong, it means the end for all those involved: I think you should know about it. There seem to be many different groups, but it is essential to get the Army on their side. Of course it is all hearsay: a word there, a hint here . . . ' At that point Paul Metternich, who was home on leave following a serious illness on the Leningrad front, came into the room. After some hesitation, Tatiana and Missie told him about the plans

The Year 1944

for a coup. He laughed and said, 'Don't look as if you've seen a ghost. This has been talked about for many months.' 'You know about it too?' they asked. 'But of course. We don't know the details, but they are trying to work them out.'[51]

In June 1944 Dulles received a confidential message through Hans-Bernd Gisevius, the German Vice-Consul in Zurich, giving advance news of the plan; and on July 12 Dulles told Washington that 'dramatic events may be impending'.

Meanwhile the military situation had taken on a new and anticipated aspect. On June 6 the Allies landed in Normandy and the German armies began to fall back. This added impetus to the moves to overthrow Hitler and, as Adam had told Christabel Bielenberg, the Germans had to do it themselves.

A few days after the Allied landings Major General Henning von Tresckow, serving on the Eastern front, and Lieutenant Fabian von Schlabrendorff were at a conference of Army commanders in East Prussia. Count Heinrich von Lehndorff arrived back from Berlin where he had met with von Stauffenberg, who sought von Tresckow's views as to whether they should proceed with plans for assassination and a coup in the light of the Allied invasion. Von Tresckow's answer was explicit:

> The assassination must be attempted at all costs. Even if it should not succeed, an attempt to seize power in Berlin must be undertaken. What matters now is no longer the practical purpose of the coup, but to prove to the world and for the records of history that the men of the resistance movement dared to take the decisive step. Compared to this objective, nothing else is of consequence.[52]

In the middle of June Adam and his wife Clarita went to meet friends in Stuttgart. On Thursday the 15th they all attended a service in the largest church in Stuttgart, the church being crowded for the late afternoon service. His wife wrote in her memoir:

> That was the last time Adam and I were together. Somehow he seemed to be more distant, difficult to reach, deeply absorbed in that which he had to do.[53]

On the 18th he had discussions with Stauffenberg and Colonel Hansen, who had replaced Canaris as head of counter intelligence. Adam was pleased with the meeting and wrote afterwards to his wife, 'It could only have been improved by your being there'. After his guests left, he wrote, 'I walked silently out to our lake under a grey clouded summer night's sky, thinking over the discussion and yours and my existence together with grateful hope'.[54] On the following day he left for his final visit to Sweden, having received a message through Frau Almstrom that the British Legation wished to talk to him. He thought that, at last, the British Government had decided to talk to, and work with, the resistance, but it was not so. No British diplomat was allowed to talk to him; instead David MacEwan, a secret service agent, interviewed him.[55] Adam gave him a memorandum for the British Government stating that, because of the insistence on unconditional surrender, he could not take the risk of naming the leaders of the opposition. (He did not know that, in May, Goerdler had disclosed names to Dulles.) He confirmed that plans for a coup were at an advanced stage and that a group of political leaders was working closely with the generals in the plot. During the visit he also met, for the first time, the future Chancellor Willy Brandt, who had left Germany in 1933; he told him of the planned coup and asked him to serve in the new government. No record is available of the discussion between Adam and MacEwan, but it is known that the British Government's decision on Adam's memorandum was that there should be no further contact.

Adam's friend and colleague, Alexander Worth, also visited Stockholm in the summer and talked with British Legation staff. It now emerged that a British decision in the sense requested by Adam and his colleagues could only be given by Churchill; and it was suggested that, if Adam could be in Stockholm for three days, he should be flown to London for an interview with Churchill. It was emphasized that the German negotiator must be Adam and Adam alone. The man who had been so suspected was now the only one to be trusted. Sadly, it was too late.

Adam von Trott had never been a physically strong man and the exertions of the past months, plus the inevitable strain of having to work clandestinely, were having their effect. On one of his last nights in Stockholm, he looked so ill that his friend Inga Kempe advised him to go back to his hotel and sleep. Inga Kempe was the sister-in-law of Heinz von Bodelschwingh, with whom Adam had been at Munich University. He called on her during his visit to Stockholm in October 1943 and she, not knowing why he was in Sweden, casually mentioned some friends at the British Legation. 'Suddenly Adam asked me if I could help him to get in touch with somebody there.' She then arranged for him to meet two political intelligence officers, the art historian, Roger Hinks, and

James Knapp-Fisher. Inga Kempe recorded Adam's reaction when she told him to get some sleep:

> He looked at me and said, 'Why should I need sleep when there is so much to do? – and besides, old people do not need so much sleep.' Whereupon I logically answered, 'But you are only thirty-five.' 'No,' said Adam, 'I am at least sixty and I will never be younger. I think I have done what I am supposed to do in my life, whatever was asked of me to do, and I am ready to die, but there are still a few things to do.' The day before he left, he told me that he had been asked by the British and the Americans not to go back to Germany, because at that moment he could do more good outside his country than inside. Then he shook his head and said, 'perhaps I could, but that is no more the question for me. I have done what I could for my country, but I also have a duty towards those who are dedicated to the same cause as I. I must share with them, whatever comes. And – there is Clarita and the children.' These were his final words.[56]

After their disillusionment at the absence of any kind of encouragement from the Allies, the resisters were at last encouraged by a speech made by Clement Attlee, Deputy Prime Minister, in the House of Commons on July 6. He appealed to them to show by active steps that they were trying to rid themselves of the Nazi regime. Attlee's intervention was inspired by Stafford Cripps, the only member of the Cabinet who was aware of the real size and potential of the German resistance movement.

The leading military activist was now Colonel Count Claus Schenck von Stauffenberg. In the early part of the war he had served with distinction in a Bavarian cavalry regiment in Poland, France and North Africa. In April 1943 he was severely wounded by fire from a low-flying Allied plane, losing one eye, his right hand, half his left hand and part of a leg. During his convalescence he revised his attitude and made no secret of his contempt for Hitler and Nazism, criticizing Hitler as the Antichrist and as the 'master of vermin'. He decided to join the conspirators with the aim of liquidating the Nazi regime and replacing it with a new social state that would maintain the good name of Germany.

Stauffenberg and Adam had possibly first met in 1938 or 1939, but their friendship only began when Stauffenberg was posted to Berlin in the late summer of 1943. From then onwards they worked closely together, although for obvious reasons they kept a low profile on their friendship. Stauffenberg was a cousin of Count Peter Yorck von

Wartenburg, through whom he became closely connected with the Kreisau Circle in which Adam was so active.

After recovering from his wounds, Stauffenberg had a number of staff appointments, culminating in June 1944 in being appointed Chief of Staff to General Fromm, Commander-in-Chief of the Reserve Army, the so-called Ersatzheer, whose second-in-command was General Friedrich Olbricht, a deeply religious man who regarded the Nazi regime as a disgrace to Germany and worked actively to overthrow it. In his new appointment Stauffenberg attended Hitler's conferences and took it upon himself that, with his frequent access to Hitler, he must be the man to kill him. He accepted Adam's pre-eminence in the political and diplomatic field and was in full agreement with the plan that, after the coup, negotiations with Russia would be carried out by Count Werner von der Schulenburg and Major-General Ernst Kostring, former Ambassador and Military Attaché respectively in Moscow, whilst those with Britain and the USA would be carried out by General Alexander von Falkenhausen, Military Governor of Belgium and Northern France, and Adam himself.

14

Final Preparations

After the success of the Allied invasion of Normandy in June, it became increasingly apparent to the German senior officers, who were now fighting a war on two fronts, that defeat was inevitable. In France the Allied forces under General Eisenhower were consolidating their early gains and preparing to move forward through France and the Low Countries into Germany itself. In the East, German troops had endured the harsh rigours of three Russian winters and now found themselves with inadequate supplies of food, clothing and equipment. Morale was low. The professional Army commanders had never trusted the Nazi Party and they now saw the removal of Hitler as the only way to end the shame and the suffering which had been brought upon the Army. It was a view shared by the Luftwaffe commanders, who felt let down by the extravagant promises of Goering, largely unfulfilled, and who had a more intimate knowledge of conditions within Germany itself. It was only in the Navy, and particularly the submarine service, that loyalty to the Nazi Party remained strong, largely owing to the fact that they were operating far from Germany and were cut off from much of the distressing news.

Two of the most senior commanders, Field Marshals von Rundstedt and Rommel, saw Hitler on June 17th and the 29th. Both tried to convince him that it would be wise to end the war while considerable German forces still existed. The dilemma faced by all German officers and soldiers was that they had taken an oath of personal loyalty to Hitler and many who wanted him overthrown found it difficult to break their oath. However, by now they had knowledge of the atrocities committed in the camps and on the Russian front; and many felt they were no longer bound to a regime which had broken the Geneva Convention and all normal codes of civilized conduct. Many senior officers had already involved themselves with the plot and some had bravely been part of the resistance movement for many years. Others now joined in. Field Marshal Erwin Rommel, the most popular of the German generals with a public acclamation equalled only by that for his old adversary, Field

Final Preparations

Marshal Sir Bernard Montgomery, in Britain was not in favour of assassination, preferring that Hitler should be arrested and put on trial. He sent a message to Hitler on July 15 which concluded:

> The troops are fighting heroically everywhere, but the unequal struggle is nearing its end. I must beg you to draw the political conclusions without delay.

Hitler did not reply and Rommel, who was never closely involved in the conspiracy, agreed to support a new regime after assassination and was designated to be Head of State. At the same time, efforts were made to gain the support of Field Marshal Gunther von Kluge, who on July 2 had become Commander-in-Chief in the West and Rommel's superior. He vacillated considerably, preferring to keep his options open like so many others, but finally he agreed to support a change of regime if the plot was successful. It was against this background of rapidly increasing disillusion with Hitler's policies and what they saw as inevitable defeat that the final preparations for the coup were made.

The task of obtaining explosives and fuses for the attempt of Hitler's life fell to Major-General Helmuth Stieff, who had obtained explosives for previous bomb attempts which had all foundered, often because Hitler so frequently changed his movements at the last moment. Despite the seriousness of the undertaking, much was done in an atmosphere that seemed almost unreal. Philipp Freiherr von Boeselager later recalled how, shortly before the attempted coup, Major-General Henning von Tresckow who led the resistance on the Eastern Front sent Philipp's brother Georg to Paris with a message for Kluge. Georg needed an excuse for making the journey. Fortunately the Boeselagers owned a racehorse named Lord Wagram which was due to run at Longchamps. It provided Georg with a perfect cover for his journey but, as Philipp remarked, it was strange that such happenings were possible at such a time of high tension.

Hitler was by now almost a recluse, rarely leaving the Berghof in Berchtesgaden, or his headquarters near Rastenburg, the so-called Wolf's Lair (Wolfsschanze), in East Prussia. On July 11th Stauffenberg attended a conference at Berchtesgaden, travelling with his adjutant, Captain Friedrich Karl Klausing. He took with him some explosives packed in a briefcase and was equipped with a pair of pliers to set the fuse, the handles of the pliers having been adapted so that he could manipulate them with his damaged hand. When he arrived, he found Himmler and Goering were not present, and as it was the intention to remove as many of the

Final Preparations

leadership as possible, he telephoned General Friedrich Olbricht and it was agreed to postpone the attempt.

Missie Vassiltchikov dined with Adam on Monday, July 10, the night before the abortive attempt and recorded in her diary:

> We spoke English to the head waiter who was delighted to show how well he still remembers it. Our neighbours began to stare. Adam then took me for a drive during which, without going into particulars, we discussed the coming events which, he told me, are now imminent. We don't see eye to eye on this, because I continue to find that too much time is being lost perfecting the details, whereas to me the one thing is really important now – the physical elimination of the man. What happens to Germany once he is dead can be seen to later. Perhaps because I am not German myself, it may all seem simpler to me, whereas for Adam it is essential that some kind of Germany be given a chance to survive.[57]

On the following Saturday, July 15, Stauffenberg flew to Hitler's headquarters at Rastenberg with General Friedrich Fromm, commander of the Reserve Army, for a conference. They had received the summons at midday on the 14th, so there was just time to activate 'Valkyrie'. ('Valkyrie' was the name given to a secret official plan, which was to be implemented in the event of a coup against the Nazi regime. The idea of the conspirators was that if they could put the plan into operation after their own coup, they would then secure the country and claim that Hitler had been assassinated in an attempted SS coup.) Everyone involved was now convinced that this was the day when it would happen. Berthold Stauffenberg commented, 'Worst of all is to know that we'll fail; and yet we must go ahead, for the sake of our country and our children.' Once again Hitler changed his movements and left the conference early, so the attempt was foiled. The initial stages of 'Valkyrie' had already been set in motion, but the conspirators managed to pass them off as an exercise.

By now Stauffenberg was depressed and the strain was beginning to tell on his nerves. He telephoned his wife Nina, now three months pregnant with their fifth child, on Sunday the 16th; it was their last conversation. On the same evening there was a meeting at the Stauffenberg brothers' home in Wannsee, halfway between Dahlem and Potsdam. Claus and Berhold Stauffenberg, Mertz von Quirnheim (Claus's successor as Chief of Staff to Olbricht), Fritz-Dietlof von der Schulenburg, Adam von Trott, Peter Yorck von Wartenburg, Casar von Hofacker (contact man with the army in France), Georg Hansen (who

Final Preparations

had succeeded Canaris at the Abwehr) and Schwerin von Schwanenfeld were present. They realized that the present situation could not continue a day longer than necessary and that the only way to save Germany was to kill Hitler as soon as possible and then seek peace negotiations with the USSR and the Allies at the same time.

On the following day, Monday the 17th, there was a meeting at Adam's flat. All seemed ready, but then came the news that Rommel's heavy open-topped Horch staff car had been unable to manoeuvre easily when it was strafed by a British plane in Normandy. Rommel had been severely wounded and put out of action for many weeks. This was a heavy blow to the conspirators and the position of post-Nazi President now reverted to General Beck.

During these tense days in Berlin Adam was having discussions with a number of people about what would happen after the coup. He was also busy calling to Berlin the people who he wanted to be at his side after the coup. He sent a telegram to Peter Bielenberg in East Prussia on Tuesday the 18th saying 'I should like to see you soon in Berlin.'[58] On the same day he sent a telegram to Missie Vassiltchikov at her office at Krummhubel, to where the Foreign office had been evacuated: 'At the office, the pre-arranged telegram from Adam: I am expected in Berlin tomorrow,' she wrote in her diary for the 18th.[59] All final arrangements were put in hand to effect a military takeover in all major centres of command – senior officers were in position in Berlin and Paris and other places who, as soon as they received notice to do so, would move troops, disarm the SS and Gestapo, arrest leading Nazis and proclaim support for the new Government.

It was with pleasure and relief that Missie Vassiltchikov left Krummhubel on Wednesday, July 19 for Berlin – 'I suspect for good. I have taken with me as little as possible. The rest will stay with Madonna Blum until I know what is to happen to me.' Her diary continues:

> Later, I had a long talk with Adam. He looks very pale and strained, but seems glad to see me. . . . The truth is that there is a fundamental difference in outlook between all of them and me: not being German, I have never attached much importance to what happens afterwards. Being patriots, they want to save their country from complete destruction by setting up some interim government, whereas I am concerned only with the elimination of the Devil. Besides, I have never believed that even such an interim government would be acceptable to the Allies, who refuse to distinguish between 'good' Germans and 'bad'. This, of course, is a fatal mistake on their part and we will probably all pay a heavy price

Final Preparations

for it. We agreed not to meet again until Friday. After he had gone, Maria Gersdorff remarked, 'I find he looks so pale and so tired; sometimes I think he is not going to live long.'[60]

On the same day, the Wednesday, Adam wrote to his wife. She kept the letter after destroying some parts of it which she memorised:

> During the next weeks and perhaps for longer, you may not hear from me at all. But what remains is deep confidence in our life together which we live at two poles, far from each other, but as part of a unity and under the same sign. I think very often and with great longing of you and the sweet children, and also of the valleys and hills, their peace, and our walks together on the high ground. Never despair in all the troubles that must surely come. They give us opportunity to recognise in fullness the gravity, the breadth and the strength of life and the Creator of life, in a way that has been denied to many generations.[61]

On the evening of Wednesday, July 19, Stauffenberg, who had worked calmly through the day, had his bomb ready; two packets of British made explosive and a British fuse. In the evening he went to Adam's flat in Dahlem and the two men had their last talk together. When he left Adam's flat, he went home to Wannsee, where he and his brother Berthold spent the rest of the evening reading their brother Alexander's latest poems (Berthold and Alexander were twins). But before he left Dahlem that evening, he went in to St Anne's Church and prayed. It was Martin Niemöller's church.

15

The 20th of July 1944

The morning sky over Berlin on Thursday, 20 July 1944 was grey and murky, the air oppressive. There was an eclipse of the sun, as if Nature itself wished to play some part in the unfolding events of the day.

Colonel Stauffenberg was to attend a conference at Hitler's headquarters at Rastenburg at 1 p.m. At 8 a.m. he left by air on the 400 mile journey, accompanied by his ADC, Lieutenant Werner von Haeften. They arrived at Rastenburg aerodrome at 10.15 a.m. At 11.30 he had a meeting with Field Marshal Wilhelm Keitel, who told him the conference was brought forward to 12.30 p.m. Stauffenberg asked for a room to freshen up; and there he and von Haeften began to repack the two bombs in his own briefcase. Before they could finish they were interrupted by a NCO with a message from General Fellgiebel, who was in the plot and whose designated duty was to close down the communications network at Rastenburg as soon as the bomb exploded. The message was not urgent, but it meant that they had no time to pack the second bomb. That was the first handicap to success, but Stauffenberg was confident that one bomb would be enough. The second problem was that, owing to building works, the meeting was not to be held in the usual concrete bunker, but in a large wooden hut, where the shock waves on which a bomb depends for its main effect would have considerably less effect. However, Stauffenberg thought if he placed the bomb close enough to Hitler, he could succeed. A third handicap was that it was a hot day and the windows were open, thus allowing some of the blast to escape.

The meeting started promptly at 12.30. On the table was a large map. Twenty four senior officers were present. A minute or two after the meeting began, Stauffenberg entered the room as General Heusinger, standing next to Hitler, was indicating the military situation on the map. Stauffenberg managed to get a place near to Hitler and placed his briefcase under the table, resting it by the table leg on the inner side to Hitler. A few minutes later he left, on the pretext of making a telephone call, leaving his cap and belt in the antechamber to imply that he would be returning. A few moments later Colonel Brandt found the briefcase to be in his way and moved it a few inches to the right, on the other side of the table leg from Hitler. At 12.45 the bomb exploded, killing among others the unfortunate Colonel Brandt who, although not part of the conspiracy, was close to many of those who were and sympathized with their aims. A year earlier he had nearly died when a bottle of brandy – which, unknown to him, contained a bomb – failed to explode in midair as Hitler and his staff were flying back to Rastenburg from the Eastern front. Hitler was not seriously wounded, having been protected by the massive table supports. Stauffenberg and von Haeften flew back to Berlin, arriving at about 3.30 p.m. and believing that Hitler was dead and all their plans for taking over the country were proceeding.

In Berlin Adam von Trott received a codeword at 2 p.m. that all plans were to be put into operation. He asked a colleague, Wilhelm Melchers, to come up to his office. Melchers later wrote:

> He was unusually pale. After I had closed the door to the outer office in which his secretary was working, he came to me, speaking softly. 'It has been done.' I stared at him speechless as he lifted his hand and made as if to fire a pistol. I asked him, 'And you have received an absolutely trustworthy report?' He answered that he had had a telephone call from the officers with the agreed message, 'The room is free'. I grabbed his hand and said, 'I still find it hard to believe that this coup has really been brought off. We will never forget 20th July.' Then he pointed to his writing table where lay a letter for signature ending with the words, 'Heil Hitler'. He laughed and said, 'I won't need to sign letters with that miserable greeting any more.'

When Melchers left Adam's office, he met a diplomat who said there had been a radio announcement of an attempt on Hitler's life, but he was safe. He returned to Adam's office. They looked out of the window to the street, which was sealed off. Central Berlin, it seemed, was being sealed off in accordance with the plan. At 6.45 p.m. came the special communiqué announcing that Hitler was unhurt. They looked out of the window again; the street was open to traffic. Adam's friend, Hans-Bernd von Haeften, constantly tried to telephone his brother who was with Stauffenberg, but there was no reply. The four men who had waited together all afternoon for the dawning of a new era – Adam, Alexander Werth (a friend from Göttingen days), Hans-Bernd von Haeften and Melchers – began to face the awful realisation that the coup had failed.

They decided to break up their meeting. Adam said he would remain in the office until 8 o'clock, although in fact he stayed until 11 p.m., hoping to hear from Stauffenberg. His wife Clarita wrote in her memoir:

> Can one find the courage to imagine what he went through in those four lonely hours in that room?[62]

When Adam finally left his office (he was using the office of State Secretary Keppler who was away) he joined Alexander Werth at the Foreign Press Club and there, at 12.30, they heard the broadcast voice of Hitler. He now knew the worst and, shortly afterwards, he and Hans-Bernd von Haeften took a night walk in the Grunewald. There they planned what they would say if either or both were arrested. For Adam it was the sad culmination not just of the plans of the last few months; it was the culmination of his resistance that had started when he first read of Hitler's appointment as Chancellor in 1933 and, indeed, even earlier when he spoke of his distaste of National Socialism at the Oxford University German Club in 1931.

When Stauffenberg arrived back in Berlin at 3.30 p.m. he found that 'Valkyrie' had not been set in motion owing to lack of clear directives and information from Rastenburg, where General Fellgiebel, Head of Army Communications and one of the conspirators, had failed to close down the communications system effectively. Stauffenberg insisted that Hitler was dead and tried to push the coup forward. Coded 'Valkyrie' orders were issued, but General Fromm, commander of the Reserve Army in Berlin, would not participate. He telephoned Keitel, who confirmed that Hitler was alive. From then on, Fromm refused to have anything to do with the coup, despite anything Stauffenberg said. Eventually, he declared the conspirators to be under arrest, whereupon Stauffenberg retorted that, on the contrary, Fromm was under arrest; he was relieved of his revolver and kept under guard. Meanwhile, the commandant of the Berlin garrison, Colonel-General Paul von Hase (uncle of the Bonhoeffers), failed to take control on behalf of the resistance. The Guard Battalion was under the command of Major Ernst Remer, who started to carry out the orders he received and to cordon off the Government quarter. Unfortunately he was in contact personally with a Nazi lieutenant, Hans Hagen, who worked in Goebbels's Propaganda Ministry. Hagen guessed from the troop movements that a coup was happening and persuaded Remer to accompany him to see Goebbels. Goebbels put Remer on the telephone to Hitler in person, who told Remer that the future of the Third Reich was in his hands and that he was responsible for security until Himmler arrived. Hitler ordered him to take over the Reserve Army; Remer was won over and the coup was doomed. The Bendlerblock (Army headquarters) was sealed off and troops were told that the orders they had previously received were unauthorised.

Although Fromm had been arrested, the conspirators merely kept him and his staff under guard. Later in the evening he was released and took control again. He arrested Stauffenberg and his companions, including General Beck who many years before had been Fromm's commander-in-chief. When they were required to hand over their arms, Beck asked 'Would you take the gun from your old commander?' Fromm relented and allowed Beck to keep his revolver. In an apparent effort to impress Hitler, Fromm then held a summary court-martial of five of the six officers he was holding; all were sentenced to death. The sixth officer, Colonel-General Erich Hoepner, was a tank commander who had been sacked and disgraced by Hitler for refusing to obey inhuman commands on the Russian front. He was an old friend of Fromm and was therefore spared to stand further trial. It was an act of supposed generosity on Fromm's part, but in the light of later events it would have been kinder if he had suffered instant execution that night. Beck asked permission to commit suicide and this was granted, but he had to do it immediately with the others in the room. Hoepner later said that Beck used his own Luger pistol, but only managed to give himself a slight head wound. In a state of extreme stress, the 64-year-old general asked for another gun and an officer gave him a Mauser. The second attempt was also unsuccessful. 'Help the old gentleman' said Fromm. A sergeant then gave Beck the coup de grace.

Stauffenberg, Mertz von Quirnheim, Olbricht and Werner von Haeften were taken to the courtyard of the Bendlerblock and shot. Haeften threw himself in front of Stauffenberg who cried out 'Long live Germany'.

It was midnight.

16

Aftermath

The day after the unsuccessful coup, on Friday, July 21, Melchers asked Adam if there were any other groups which might be successful. 'No, there is no hope,' said Adam, 'and none for the future. It is all finished now and we will have to suffer the consequences. No stone will be left unturned. Hitler will continue this stupid war – the real nihilist that he is – until everything has been destroyed.' He added he was pleased the plot had taken place – it was a historical fact and that was at least something.[63]

Over the next few days, friends tried to persuade Adam to escape. Count Berg (an army officer on the staff of Field Marshal von Kluge) urged him to go with him to France, but he refused. Franz-Josef Furtwängler (a trade union official who was a fringe member of the Kreisau Circle) knew of a way to Switzerland via his home village on the German–Swiss border, but he said to Furtwängler, 'I shall take the blame for everything. Have you still got a copy of our paper "Germany between East and West"? It would be a pity if it were to get lost. You will see that everything will turn out as we predicted.' Waltraud von Götz (Adam's cousin) knew how to get him to Poland. He refused them all, saying, 'I shall take the blame.' Perhaps the most moving statement on what had happened was made by Major-General Henning von Tresckhow, serving on the Eastern front. He telephoned his friend Fabian von Schlabrendorff and, in a completely calm voice, said:

> Now the whole world will fall on us and curse us. But I hold to the firm opinion that we did the right thing. I hold Hitler to be not only the arch fiend of Germany, but the arch fiend of the whole world. In a few hours I shall stand before God's judgment seat, to lay before him my sins of commission and omission, and I know I will stand by my good conscience in the matter of what I undertook against Hitler. God once promised Abraham that he would spare Sodom if ten just men could be found there. So I hope that God will spare Germany because

we stood firm for our country. Not one of us can complain that we must die. Everyone who joined the conspiracy put on the shirt of Nessus. The moral worth of a man only shows itself when he is prepared to die for what he believes in.[64]

Then he explained everything to Major Kuhn, commander of the 28th Commando Division which he was visiting that day. He went in to no man's land, where he mimicked an exchange of fire with two pistols, so that Kuhn could report he had died in action. Once out of sight, he took a rifle grenade, pulled the safety pin, and blew himself up.

Two days after the plot attempt, on the Saturday, Missie Vassiltchikov found an opportunity to talk to Adam:

On entering Judgie Richter's office this morning, I found the older Haeften, Hans-Bernd (our former Chief of Personnel), sitting at his desk eating cherries out of a paper bag. And his brother shot the day before yesterday like a dog! He smiled to me and chatted as if nothing had happened.

I went down to Adam's room. I found him with one of his assistants, who soon left. Adam threw himself down on a sofa and, pointing to his neck, said 'I'm in it up to here.' He looked dreadful. We talked in whispers. The sight of him made me unhappier still. I told him so. He said yes, but to me it was merely as if I had lost the favourite tree in my orchard, whereas for him it's everything he had hoped for that was gone. The intercom rang: our boss, Dr Six, wanted to see him. We agreed to meet in the evening. When I went over to Maria Gersdorff, I told her how anxious I was about Adam. 'But why?' she asked. 'He knew Stauffenberg only slightly, didn't he? No, I'm certain he is not deeply involved!' – 'No,' I said, 'not really involved at all.'

I then went over to the Adlon where I was meeting Loremarie Schonburg and Aga. We assembled at Aga's and had tea on the lawn. Then Adam joined us. He had been with Dr Six, trying to put him off the scent. He looked like death. I drove back with him to his house and sat on the balcony in the sun while he changed. When Adam reappeared we sat outside and he told me about some of it.

Stauffenberg, he said, was a wonderful man, not only brilliantly intelligent but also with exceptional vitality and drive. If only it had been somebody who could fire a gun, the attempt might have succeeded. But Stauffenberg was too badly disabled. He has lost in him, Adam said, his closest friend. He seemed completely crushed.

Adam himself had spent the whole day of the 20th at the A.A. in the

Wilhelmstrasse, waiting for the military takeover. He said he knew he would be arrested, he was too deeply compromised.

Adam wondered aloud whether he should not have a piece published in the London Times, explaining what these men represented. He went on to tell me that shortly after France fell in 1940, he received a letter from his old friend Lord Lothian (at the time British Ambassador in Washington) in which the latter urged him to work for a reconciliation between Germany and England. Whether Lothian had in mind only a non-Nazi Germany (he knew of Adam's hatred of the regime) was not clear. But to Adam the thought of any possible 'deal' between the two countries while Hitler was still at the helm was so odious, that he never mentioned the existence of the letter to anyone. Afterwards he often wondered whether he had not been wrong.

We sat up all night talking and listening to stray sounds outside and every time we heard a car slowing down, I could see on his face what he was thinking. Adam said Alex Worth knows all and if he is arrested, Alex would know what to do. He thinks that Dr Six suspects something too, as he keeps pressing Adam to go to Switzerland. I, also, insisted that he should go – immediately. But no, he will not, because of his wife and children. He said that if they arrested him, he would deny everything – in order to get out and try again.[65]

Otto John, a lawyer at Lufthansa, was involved in the Lufthansa Administration/Abwehr/Foreign Office axis of the resistance. In his account of the events of July 20 and after, he said:

On the Sunday I went to see Trott who knew that my work for the Lufthansa allowed me to carry an Army permit to travel whenever I liked. With him was Bielenberg. They both urged me to leave Berlin while there was still time to do so and, as Trott put it, 'tell the world what it was we had wanted to achieve and why we had failed.'

I agreed to go, and asked Trott to come with me, but he refused on account of his family. The following day, Monday 24th July, I left for Madrid by Lufthansa on the routine flight. I had no trouble at all leaving Germany.[66]

Throughout the days following the coup attempt, Adam was expecting arrest at any moment. On the Friday evening, 21st, he had walked in the Grunewald with Waltraud von Goetz. He told her that he felt like a tree that had been deprived of its branches, referring to the friends whom he had lost already. He thought the ultimate reason for the failure was Britain's refusal to co-operate. 'Deep down, he did not believe in his own survival.' He told her he intended to write a political testament; he seems to have done so and to have hidden it somewhere near Peter Bielenberg's house in Berlin,[67] but it has never been discovered.

Curt Bley, a former socialist student leader whom Adam first met in 1932 and who was active in the resistance movement, was not personally involved in the plot. When he heard of it, he guessed Adam was part of it and he therefore went immediately to Berlin. Adam told him of the events of the past few days and said, 'I do not fear death. I fear only the humiliations I shall have to face on the way to the scaffold.' They bade goodbye to each other on the doorstep of Adam's house on the morning of Tuesday, July 25.

Adam attended the daily meeting at the main A.A. office in the Wilhelmstrasse that morning. Whilst he was there, the Gestapo walked in to his office and demanded to know his whereabouts. His secretary tried to get away to warn him, but they restrained her. He walked straight into the trap and was arrested at noon. Missie Vassiltchikov had telephoned him at home early and found he was still all right. Later in the morning, she called at his office, but only his secretary was there, with a scared expression. Missie went for a quick lunch and returned to Adam's office. The secretary – 'a nice girl and a friend' – tried to prevent her entering Adam's room, but she pushed past her. 'At his desk a small man in civilian clothes was going through his drawers. Another one lounged in an armchair. When we had left the room, she looked at me beseechingly and put her finger to her lips.'[68] Colonel Stauffenberg's driver's logbooks had recorded the number of times that his employer called on Adam at Dahlem and it is likely that this was the lead that took the Gestapo to Adam's office.

Many of those arrested were tortured during interrogation by the Gestapo, but fortunately nothing is known of the circumstances in which Adam was questioned. Records of the interrogation sessions were kept; it appears that the Gestapo did not realize how deeply he was involved in the plot. In fact, they knew very little about his activities – nothing of his dealings in America, Switzerland, Belgium or Holland, and nothing about some of his meetings in Sweden. Their accusations centred round his friendship with Stauffenberg and their frequent meetings. This was, of course, sufficient to incriminate him in an atmosphere of terror where the slightest acquaintance with anyone, or a name in an address book, or a telephone number on a piece of paper, or any other such routine 'evidence' could lead to immediate arrest and accusation. For the Gestapo, the knowledge of his friendship with Stauffenberg, plus the fact that he did not conceal his opinion that the war was lost, proved that he must have known of, and been involved in, the plans for assassination. The deduction was correct, but there was no proof. During his interrogations he carefully attributed blame only to those he knew were dead or out of danger. He told them of his journeys abroad, stressing his role in negotiations with the Allies; this gave the SS the opportunity of using him as a negotiator if they wished to conclude a separate peace. He mentioned Weizsacker as the leader of the opposition, knowing that he was safe in the Vatican. He suggested that Stauffenberg had been in contact with Eisenhower's representative and had acquired certain information – although he knew the information had been brought by Otto John and he was not sure that John was completely safe from the Gestapo in Spain. On July 29, Missie Vassiltchikov recorded Adam's position as being 'stationary'[69] and his friends were still hoping that he might be freed, although they realized how serious his position was. On 27th July she learned that a list had been found listing members of the proposed new government, in which Adam was to be Under Secretary of State for Foreign Affairs. The existence of several lists, drawn up by different people, led to many arrests. Some of the leaders, including it is thought, Stauffenberg, would have preferred Adam to be Foreign Secretary, although others thought Ulrich von Hassell would have that position.

Peter Bielenberg, who had learned of Adam's arrest from the factory he managed in Grandenz in East Prussia, spoke to Missie on 3rd August of a plan to rescue him. He said Adam was imprisoned outside Berlin and was brought with a one-man escort each morning in an ordinary car to Gestapo headquarters for questioning. He and Alexander Werth would ambush the car and smuggle Adam into Poland, where Polish partisans would look after him. 'What a relief to hear somebody ready to act and willing to take on even the SS!' she wrote in her diary. On the same morning as he outlined his plan, Loremarie Schonburg told Missie that on one of her visits to the Gestapo headquarters in the Prinz Albrechtstrasse, where she had a contact from whom she was trying to get information about Adam, she had passed him in a corridor.

> His hands were manacled, he was evidently being led to interrogation; he recognised her but looked straight through her. The expression on his face, she said, was that of somebody already in another world. They are surely being tortured.[70]

When Bielenberg returned to his factory on August 6 to collect weapons from the armoury, he found the Gestapo waiting for him and he was arrested. He had been betrayed by his own secretary, who had taken to the Gestapo the telegram sent to him by Adam on July 18, which stated, 'I should like to see you soon in Berlin.'

Adam stood trial in the Volksgerichthof (People's Court) on August 15 with Hans-Bernd von Haeften, Count Wolf Heinrich von Helldorff (former Police President of Berlin) and three others. The whole of the trial was filmed. Adam stood with composure, his hands folded in front of him, before the dreaded Judge Freisler. As Freisler shouted, so Adam quietly answered the questions. As he sat between two guards, his expression seems to be one of defiance. There was no real evidence against him and Freisler merely mocked his war service and his Oxford education. The prosecution's case was based solely on his friendship with Stauffenberg which he could not deny. When Freisler asked him if he was aware that his participation in discussions was tantamount to attempted assassination, Adam replied calmly, 'Gewiss' – 'Certainly'. Baron Anton Saurma von der Jeltsch (Tony Saurma) was present at the trial. On August 24 he told Missie about it:

> Adam had caught sight of him, had made no sign of recognition, had looked at him fixedly for a long time and had then started to sway back and forth from the waist in a rocking kind of movement. He wore no tie, was clean-shaven and very pale. He (Tony) had gone out before the verdict was read out as he knew from the start what it would be.[71]

All received the anticipated death sentence. The other five were executed immediately, but Adam was spared for another eleven days. In the Gestapo reports a note was entered: 'Since Trott has obviously withheld a good deal, the death sentence delivered by the Volksgerichthof has not been carried out, so that he may be available for further clarification.'

Adam's chief, Dr Six, asked his assistant, Dr Horst Mahnke and another high-ranking officer named Dr Schmidz to draft a letter to Himmler soon after Adam's arrest. In the letter it was stated that, although the arrested men from the Auswartige Amt could be assumed to be guilty, it might be prudent to replace the anticipated death sentences by sentences of imprisonment because in the negotiations to be expected (when the war finished) there would be need of personalities who were known abroad. As early as 1942 Himmler had asked his Finnish masseur, when speaking of Hitler, 'What do you think? Is the man mad?' Certainly, Himmler had for some long time before 1945 been tentatively planning to replace Hitler if he could secure some kind of peace terms –

although the Allies would never have negotiated with a man of Himmler's record. Stalingrad shook Himmler's faith in Hitler still further and by early 1944, Dr Six was seeking on Himmler's behalf to put out feelers to the Allies. It was therefore not surprising that when Himmler received the letter from Dr Six suggesting that, when sentences of death were passed on Adam and Hans-Bernd von Haeften, they might be commuted to imprisonment, Himmler himself agreed. He in turn put the proposition to Hitler, but he is reported to have thrown a tantrum – a tobsuchtanfall – screaming that the Foreign Office men must all be hanged. Himmler did not raise the matter again. Apart from the fact that Adam's contacts with leading personalities in Britain and elsewhere were already well known, perhaps it also indicates that the way he reacted to questioning after arrest, stressing his negotiating position and skills, did impress the SS. He was playing for time and to a small extent succeeded.

On August 15 Clarita von Trott went to the court, hoping to attend the trial so that Adam would see her, but permission was refused. Two days earlier her two children, Verena aged two and a half, and Clarita aged nine months had been taken away from Imshausen by Nazi officials. On the 16th and 17th she applied unsuccessfully for permission to see her husband. On the 18th she was arrested.

On the day of his trial Adam wrote to his wife:

You will know . . . that what hurts me most is that I may never again be able to place my experience at the service of this country. I wanted to use those special abilities which I have been able to develop . . . I should like so much to be able to make some sort of summary of my ideas and proposals which might help other people, but I don't suppose that it will be possible now. It was all an attempt, arising out of the love for my country (for which I must thank my father) and from the knowledge of her strength, to protect her immutable rights in the changes and chances of the modern world. I wished to preserve her profound and indispensable contribution to civilisation against the encroachment of powers and beliefs foreign to her. That is why I always hurried back eagerly from foreign countries with all their enticements and opportunities to this one which I felt I was called to serve. What I have learned and what I was able to do for Germany abroad would certainly have helped a good deal now, because there are so few people who have enjoyed such diverse opportunities in the last years as I have. So I must hope that even without me, understanding and assistance will be forthcoming from many of these connections, should it ever be wanted or necessary. But the sower would rather not leave his seed for others to care for; between the sowing and the harvest there are so many storms.[72]

Adam was in prison for four weeks and four days. Throughout that time his friends made untiring efforts trying to devise ways of saving his life. They hoped that, with his skill in dealing with questions, he might yet be acquitted; if that were not possible, they hoped that the war might end in time for him to be released. Missie Vassiltchikov tried, through a friend, to get an interview with Goebbels – 'I will move heaven and earth to get Adam and Gottfried out, and Count Schulenburg too, if need be.' When she saw her friend on August 24th, Missie told her, 'It's my boss,' adding that he had been condemned to death but was, she suspected, still alive; she would tell Goebbels that Germany could not afford to destroy so many exceptionally gifted men who could be of such use to their country. Her friend, a film star who knew Goebbels but had quarrelled with him, persuaded her to drop the idea because Goebbels was 'a cruel, vicious little sadist, with a hatred for all those involved in the attempt on Hitler's life.'

Eleven days after his trial, on the morning of Saturday, August 26, Adam was allowed to write two letters, one to his wife and one to his mother. The letters, together with the one of August 15, were delivered six months later, in February.

Beloved Claritchen,
This is, almost certainly, the very last of my letters. I hope that you got my previous longer one.

Before all else, forgive me for the deep sorrow that I have had to cause you.

Rest assured that I am still with you in thought and that I die in profound trust and faith.

Today there is a clear 'Peking sky' and the trees are rustling. Teach our dear sweet little ones to be grateful for these signs from God, and for the deeper ones, but in an active and valiant spirit.

I love you very much. There is still so much to write to you – but there is no more time.

May God keep you – I know that you will not let yourself be defeated and will struggle through to a life where I shall be standing by your side in spirit, even when you seem to be all alone. I pray for strength for you – and do the same for me, I beg. In these days I have read the Purgatorio, Maria Stuart, and Jürg Jenatsch which strangely moved me. Otherwise I have had few things of this kind, but much within me which I have been able to think about quietly and make clear to myself. So do not grieve too much on my account – essentially all is clear to me even if deeply painful. I wish I could know what the practical effects of all this are for you. Whether you want to go to Reinbek or stay (at Imshausen). They will surely surround you with love, my dearest little wife. In my former letter I asked you to give my greetings to all our many friends; I have this at heart. You know just who they are and will give the messages correctly without my help.

I embrace you with all my soul and know that you are with me.

God bless you and the little ones.

In steadfast love

Your Adam

Give Werner and Heini the same trust that they gave me in love and loyalty. Greet Imshausen and its hills from me.

Your Adam[73]

Dearest Mother,

Thank God I have the opportunity to write you a short note. You have always been very near to me, and you are now. In gratitude I cling hard to that bond which has bound us together for ever. God has been merciful to me in these weeks and has sent me joyous, clear strength for everything, or almost everything – and He has taught me where and how I failed. I ask your forgiveness above all for imposing on you this great sorrow, and that I must not be there to support you in your old age.

Tell Werner that he too has become very close to me in these last weeks and that had we seen each other again I would have gone back on every step that led to our estrangement and would have had a deep and fruitful reconciliation with him. To him and to his chivalrous care I commend my beloved Clarita and the sweet little ones, of whom I saw so little, and I ask him to extend his protection to their individuality and their freedom to find their own way of life. Stand by them in all their need!

I ask this of Heini too – in love and gratitude.

To you last a grateful kiss from the heart until we meet again.

A greeting to all who can remember me without rancour.

Your son who loves you very much

Adam[74]

In the afternoon he was hanged in the Plotzensee Prison in Berlin. He was thirty-five years old.

Aftermath

On September 12 the news was reported in *The Times* and *The Daily Telegraph*. Sir Stafford Cripps revealed that the British Government had known of Adam's arrest and had been making indirect representations on his behalf. Having consistently failed to give any recognition or encouragement to Adam and his friends in their attempts to overthrow Hitler and the Nazi regime, they interceded when it was too late.

Dr Harold Poelchau was the Protestant chaplain at the Tegel prison, where most of the prisoners were held. He was himself a member of the Kreisau Circle, with a long record of opposition to the Nazis. Remarkably he was never suspected by the Gestapo. It fell to him to minister to many of his friends and colleagues in the closing days of their lives and to be with them until shortly before they went to their deaths. On August 26 he visited Clarita in her cell. She guessed what he had come to say.

17

The Allied Reaction

The British and Americans appeared completely surprised by the attempted coup, in spite of all the information that had come from Sweden and Switzerland in the previous two years. Cadogan expressed complete surprise in his diary. Churchill was visiting Montgomery's headquarters in Normandy. When Montgomery gave him the news, he asked Montgomery and Brigadier (later Sir) Edgar Williams to go through his dispatch boxes, where they found Ultra signals and intelligence reports unsorted and muddled up. Many years later Edgar Williams recalled how he saw that Field Marshal von Witzleben was involved; he had already been told by a senior Nazi deserter that Witzleben was the likely leader of the coup against Hitler. He told how:

> I suddenly realised that Winston had come from London with all this stuff in his dispatch box unread and that he was 'naked' in face of the possible sudden end of the war. I was amazed that he could have been as unbriefed about what was going on in Germany as he was on 21st July.[75]

Allied policy towards Germany was debated in the House of Commons on 2 August 1944. At the end of a long speech, Churchill referred to the attempted coup of July 20:

> Not only are those once proud German armies being beaten back on every front and by every one of the many nations who are in fighting contact with them, every single one, but in their homeland in Germany tremendous events have occurred which must shake to their foundations the confidence of the people and the loyalty of the troops. The highest personalities in the German Reich are murdering one another, or trying to, while the avenging armies of the Allies close upon the doomed and ever-narrowing circle of their power. Important as may be

The Allied Reaction

these manifestations of internal disease, decisive as they may be one of these days, it is not in them that we should put our trust, but in our own strong arms and the justice of our cause.[76]

It was unusual for Churchill not to pay tribute to opponents where it was deserved – in a debate seeking a Vote of Confidence in the House of Commons on 27 January 1942, he had said of Rommel:

We have a very daring and skilful opponent against us and, may I say across the havoc of war, a great general.[77]

Perhaps he regretted his 1944 speech, for in 1946 he paid generous tribute to those who died in the attempt to overthrow Hitler:

In Germany there lived an opposition which was weakened by their losses and an enervating international policy, but which belongs to the noblest and greatest that the political history of any nation has ever produced. These men fought without help from within or from abroad – driven forward only by the restlessness of their conscience. As long as they lived they were invisible and unrecognizable to us, because they had to camouflage themselves. But their death made the resistance visible.[78]

When Fabian von Schlabrendorff, who had visited Churchill in the early summer of 1939, returned to Chartwell in 1949, Churchill told him that during the war he had been misled 'by his assistants about the considerable strength and size of the anti-Hitler resistance.'[79]

Unlike Churchill, Anthony Eden (Foreign Secretary) never gave any post-war recognition to the German resistance movement. In his Memoirs published in 1965 the only references are in two extracts from his diary:

1944, July 20th: Difficult meeting of Armistice and Post-War Committee in afternoon. This was followed by Cabinet, during which I got news of attempt on Hitler's life. Ernie B. (Bevin) at once said that it was Nazi stunt to popularize H. Brendan (Bracken) said it was Goebbels' work. I said it was hard to tell so far, but I didn't think so. July 21st: House in morning when I dealt with a number of questions on business and declined to speak of Germany. Quite sure that my diagnosis of H. (Hitler) business was right and that there has been some real trouble in Germany.[80]

The Allied Reaction

In the Foreign Office the German desk continued to belittle the plotters. Wheeler-Bennett, the Deputy Head of Political Warfare, sent the following astonishing memorandum to Eden and Churchill on July 25:

1. Within the narrow limits of our accurate information it is not possible to make a certain appreciation of the position resulting from the recent events in Germany, and to deduce certain future developments from it.
2. It may now be said with some definiteness that we are better off with things as they are today than if the plot of July 20th had succeeded and Hitler been assassinated. In this event the 'Old Army' Generals would have taken over and, as may be deduced from the recent statement from the Vatican as to the Pope's readiness to mediate, would have put into operation through Baron von Weizsacker a peace move, already prepared, in which Germany would admit herself defeated and would sue for terms other than those of Unconditional Surrender.
3. By the failure of the plot we have been spared the embarrassments, both at home and in the United States, which might have resulted from such a move and, moreover, the present purge is presumably removing from the scene numerous individuals which might have caused us difficulty, not only had the plot succeeded, but also after the defeat of a Nazi Germany.
4. If it is true that a number of the more distinguished generals, together with such civilians as Schacht, Neurath and Schulenberg, have been eliminated, the Gestapo and the S.S. have done us an appreciable service in removing a selection of those who would undoubtedly have posed as 'good' Germans after the war, while preparing for a third World War. It is to our advantage therefore that the purge should continue, since the killing of Germans by Germans will save us from future embarrassments of many kinds.[81]

This memorandum, expressing implicit approval of the continuance of the purge, was sent on the very day when Adam returned from a conference to his office and walked into the arms of the Gestapo.

A more reasoned argument was put forward a week later in a minute from Thomas Marshall, Head of the Foreign Office Research Unit on Germany (which, ironically, was based at Balliol College). He pointed out that the failure of the plot had not eliminated the possibility of a non-Nazi German Government seeking a negotiated peace and the Allies should be clear as to what their attitude would be if such a peace were sought. He continued:

> I do not agree that the failure of the plot is to our advantage, especially if it is going to lead, among other things, to the murder of prisoners of war.
>
> If all internal attempts to overthrow Hitler fail, we shall have no German Government with which to deal when the end comes. There will be a state of anarchy in Germany. Consequently it may well be argued that any revolution is to our advantage, provided we do not allow it to weaken our purpose.[82]

Oliver Harvey, Assistant Under-Secretary, wrote in his diary on July 30:

> I am convinced that it was to our interest that this coup has failed. If Hitler had died, we should have had a surge to make peace with the generals – the rot must proceed further yet. Our enemies are both the Nazis and the generals. We should make peace with neither.

On the night of July 20th Carleton Greene, head of BBC German language broadcasts, was asked to write a news report about the attempt on Hitler's life for broadcasting to the German people and the rest of Europe. Assuming that some of the conspirators might be in hiding in various parts of Germany (which was so), he started with the words, 'Civil war has broken out in Germany.' A few hours later he was told that his broadcast was not favoured by the Foreign Office, who wanted the BBC to follow a much more hostile attitude to the leaders of the coup. The next day, the Political Warfare Executive issued a directive about propaganda to be broadcast to Germany on 'the Revolt of the Generals':

> Do not express or imply Allied support for, or commendation of the dissidents as 'good Germans' or suggest any possibility of a negotiated peace, or indeed any deviation from the Prime Minister's last statement. Our line is still 'unconditional surrender' from competent representatives of Germany and the Wehrmacht. The only question for the German people is whether it comes sooner or later.

It was, in fact, misleading to refer constantly to 'the revolt of the generals', because the Foreign Office had known for some years of the close involvement of civilians, including politicians, civil servants, churchmen and lawyers. Above all, Adam's visits to neutral countries, and the messages he sent to Britain, were proof of an opposition embracing many segments of German national life.

18

The Military Situation

Before the bomb exploded at Rastenburg on July 20th, Germany's military commanders already knew that the war was lost. Rommel had opened a radio link with the Americans at the end of June; on July 2 there was a four hours truce at Sept Vents and eight German nurses from Cherbourg were passed through the lines; on July 9 German envoys were fed at the American forward headquarters whilst two German nurses and seven women secretaries were handed over. Also on 9th July General Karl Stuelpnagel, Military Commander of Paris and one of the most active plotters, together with his aide Colonel Caesar von Hofacker (a cousin of Stauffenberg) visited Rommel at his headquarters at La Roche Guyon. Rommel (who preferred that Hitler should be arrested and put on trial rather than assassinated) said the military situation was hopeless and, on the day the coup took place, he would ask Montgomery for an armistice. Rommel and Stuelpnagel then instructed Walter Bargatzky, a lawyer on Stuelpnagel's staff, to draft a surrender document which Rommel could send to Montgomery. The document comprised a simple request to Montgomery for 'initial secrecy' and 'honourable treatment' of German troops after the surrender. On the 16th and 17th July Rommel told some of his commanders that there was the likelihood of an armistice. On the 17th July Rommel was severely wounded.

With Rommel out of action, much depended on Field Marshal von Kluge. Although he was a party to the plot, he vacillated and only agreed to join it fully if it was successful. However, when he heard the false news that Hitler was dead on the 20th, he said to one of his staff officers, 'If the Fuehrer is dead, we ought to get in touch with the people on the other side at once.' If he had done so, it is unlikely that a request for an armistice would have been refused; both sides were locked in a major tank battle south of Caen, with very heavy casualties, of which the outcome was uncertain.

On August 15, the day on which Adam stood on trial before the People's Court, Kluge disappeared and was out of contact with his staff

The Military Situation

all day. They tried in vain to contact him by radio; nobody knew where he was, but at Hitler's headquarters an Allied radio signal was picked up, asking where Kluge was. After the war his son-in-law said that Kluge 'went to the front lines, but was unable to get in touch with the Allied commanders.' Also in mid-August, the American General Patton disappeared from his headquarters for a whole day, saying on his return that a German emissary he was to meet had not arrived at the appointed place.

Although the official Allied policy was still 'unconditional surrender', Eisenhower had been authorized by Roosevelt and Churchill to accept a battlefield surrender, which would have involved Kluge in leaving all his guns and heavy equipment in Normandy and withdrawing his troops to Germany. Rommel's own preference was to offer Montgomery an immediate battlefield surrender (Eisenhower was still at Portsmouth) and, while the new Government negotiated a peace settlement with the three major allies, German troops would be withdrawn from all occupied territories in the west.

If the coup had succeeded on July 20, it seems likely that there would have been a surrender within a few days and the war would have been over. The failure of the coup, and the consequent collapse of surrender plans, meant that the war in Europe was to last for another ten months; and more people died (military and civilian) in the final year of the war than in the previous five years.

It is a measure of how much hinged on the plot and of how great was the prize for which Adam von Trott and his friends risked, and gave, their lives.

19

Epilogue

By 20 July 1944 Adam's mission in life was, in a sense, complete. For many years he had walked with destiny, knowing the dangers in what he was doing, but convinced that it was the only course for him to follow. He had said himself that he had done all he set out to do; if the plot succeeded, he would be there to serve his country, and the wider community of nations, in a new and, hopefully, peaceful world; if it failed, he and his friends would at least have shown the world that there were many Germans who wanted to purge their country of the evil forces that had taken control of it.

He was a man of outstanding intellectual gifts, but at the same time a man of humility who mixed easily with people of all walks of life; a man who could be moved with compassion at the death of his secretary – 'a nice, harmless, very loyal little person'. Among his staff he was always popular and Tatiana Metternich has described how he went about his work at his office:

> We realised that the personality of Adam Trott, quite apart from his striking good looks, stood out in stark relief beside all those around him. For he was such a many-sided man, in search of a challenge and a meaning in all things. He could not accept the fact that the Allies had embarked on a crusade against Germany without making any distinction between Nazis and non-Nazis.
>
> He was always happier when speaking English, as if it brought on pleasant, lighter memories. He had studied in England and had many friends there, but although he spoke the language perfectly, the rhythm of his thought was German. He usually sat, lazily draped in easy grace over his hard office armchair, dictating at a leisurely pace. But he could suddenly switch to intense concentration, for he had an untiring capacity for work. Always direct in his dealings with people, he would listen with great attention, feeling for the colour of their thoughts. If no headway could be made, he asked ironic questions in a gentle voice.[83]

Epilogue

It will never be known what Adam's thoughts were as he languished in his cell after his arrest on July 25th, and particularly in the eleven days between the sentence and execution. It is reasonable to assume that he would have thought back over his short life; and that among those thoughts would have been the memories of his many sojourns in the England he loved and the people he knew there; particularly, perhaps, his student days in Oxford – the city which he said in a letter to his father was 'of an almost miraculous beauty in its summer stillness. It has given me more perhaps than I shall ever be able to tell'. It was a time that meant so much to him and later in his life he used to tell his wife Clarita about his life at Mansfield and Balliol.

Adam's life was a comparatively short one, but it encompassed some of the most momentous events of the twentieth century. Having resolved to oppose the Nazi regime from its earliest days, he never wavered from his chosen path, although he knew that if he and his friends failed in their final objective, one certain fate awaited them. When they pleaded for some kind of recognition, some small encouragement, from the Allies, their pleas were met with silence, derision and even hostility. Undeterred, they pressed on –

That which we are, we are;
One equal temper of heroic hearts,
Made weak by time and fate, but strong in will
To strive, to seek, to find, and not to yield.[84]

The events of the 20th of July 1944 are often referred to as 'the failed plot'. To the extent that Hitler survived, the description is true, but failure does not always deny success; and Adam von Trott had succeeded, along with his many friends, in showing the world that purity of motive, loyalty to conscience and the willingness to sacrifice one's own life for the greater good of mankind are virtues which ultimately triumph over the tragedy of the moment.

Short Biographies

General Ludwig Beck, Chief of Army General Staff, 1935–1938, after which he became leader of resistance in Armed Forces. Designated Head of State if 1944 plot had been successful. Committed suicide in the Bendlerstrasse on the evening of 20 July 1944.

Dr George Kennedy Allen Bell, Bishop of Chichester, friend of Dietrich Bonhoeffer and thereby a principal contact for Britain with the German resistance. On 9 February 1944, he made a major speech in the House of Lords on the Government's bombing policy, pleading for an end to saturation bombing.

Dietrich Bonhoeffer, evangelical pastor and theologian. University chaplain in Berlin before the war, pastor in London. After returning to Germany from USA in 1939, worked with resistance groups. Arrested on 5 April 1943 and therefore not involved in planning of 1944 plot. Transferred to Buchenwald concentration camp on 7 February 1945 and later to Flossenburg where he was executed on 9 April 1945.

Admiral Wilhelm Canaris, head of the Abwehr and an important link in the Army–Secret Service–Foreign Office grouping. Hanged at Flossenburg on 9 April 1945.

Sir Stafford Cripps, friend of Adam von Trott from Oxford days. Partly financed his stay in the Far East as part of his Rhodes Scholarship. Served in various Labour Governments. British Ambassador to Russia 1940–1942. Supported pleas from German resistance group within British Cabinet, but to no avail.

General Alexander von Falkenhausen, Military Commander in Belgium and Northern France, 1940–1944. Imprisoned in various concentration camps after his dismissal. Although not actively involved in the 1944 plot, he knew of the plans from Adam von Trott and kept the information confidential. Died 1966.

Short Biographies

General Fritz Erich Fellgiebel, head of Army Communications. A key figure in the July 20th plot. Executed 4 September 1944.

Roland Freisler, became President of the People's Court in August 1942. Prisoner of war in Russia during World War 1, then a Bolshevik commissar. Returned to Germany and studied law. Known as 'the hanging judge', Hitler referred to him as 'our Vyshinsky'. At noon on February 3rd 1945, just as he was beginning to hear the case against Fabian von Schlabrendorff, a very heavy raid by American bombers began on Berlin. The court building received a direct hit and Freisler was killed when a heavy beam struck him on the head.

General Friedrich Fromm, commander of the Reserve Army. Executed for cowardice on Hitler's orders after July 20 plot.

Dr Carl Friedrich Goerdler, former Mayor of Leipzig. Chief of Conservative Civilian Resistance. Chancellor-Elect if 1944 coup had succeeded. Executed at Plotzensee Prison on 2 February 1945.

Lieutenant Werner von Haeften, Claus Stuffenberg's ADC. Shot at midnight on 20 July 1944.

Lieutenant Hans-Bernd von Haeften, lawyer in Foreign Office. Involved in resistance, but opposed to assassination of Hitler. Executed 15 August 1944. Brother of Werner von Haeften.

General Franz Halder, Chief of Army General Staff 1938–1942, leader of planned Army coup in 1938. Put into concentration camp after 20 July plot, freed shortly before he was to be executed.

Lieutenant Ludwig Freiherr von Hammerstein, Beck's ADC in the event of a successful coup. Escaped from the Bendlerblock on 20 July 1944 and survived the war.

General Paul von Hase, uncle of Bonhoeffer, Commandant of the Berlin garrison 1940–1944. Executed on 8 August 1944.

Ulrich von Hassell, lawyer and diplomat. Ambassador in Rome 1932–1938. Involved in negotiations with Vatican and drew up plans for future of Germany with Beck, Goerdler and their group. Executed 8 September 1944.

Short Biographies

Wolf Heinrich Graf von Helldorf, Prefect of Police for Berlin from 1935. Upbraded his officers for obeying orders to do nothing on 'Kristallnacht'. Executed 5 August 1944.

General Erich Hoepner, tank commander who was dismissed and disgraced by Hitler for refusing to obey inhuman commands on Russian front. Senior member of military resistance. Executed 8 August 1944.

William Adolf Visser't Hooft, World Alliance of YMCAs, based in Geneva. Met Adam von Trott in September 1928 and remained in contact with him. Acted as conduit between resistance movement in Germany and British Government.

Wilfrid Israel, manager of large Jewish family department store in Berlin. From 1933 to 1938 was instrumental in arranging for many Jews to leave Germany. Came to England in 1938 and worked for Foreign Research and Press Service. Died when civilian aeroplane was shot down in June 1943.

Otto John, lawyer at Lufthansa. Active in resistance. Flew to Madrid on Monday 24 July 1944 and survived the war.

Field Marshal Wilhelm Keitel, Chief of High Command of Armed Forces 1938 to 1945. Hitler' closest military adviser. Sentenced to death at Nuremberg trials and executed on 16 October 1946.

Field Marshal Hans Gunther von Kluge, vacillated in his support for the resistance. Became commander-in-chief in the West in July 1944. Dismissed on 18 August because he failed to report the plot and was suspected of seeking to negotiate with the Western Allies. Committed suicide on 19 August 1944.

Field Marshal Erich von Manstein, Commander-in-Chief on Eastern Front 1942–1944 when he was dismissed for urging retreat. Refused to turn against Hitler because of his loyalty oath.

Helmuth James Graf von Moltke, lawyer in Berlin in 1934 and practised law in Britain from 1935 to 1938. Peace mission to London in 1939. Owned the Kreisau estate in Silesia and was a leader of the Kreisau Circle. Executed 23 January 1945.

Short Biographies

Martin Niemöller, evangelical minister and founder member of church resistance to Nazi government. A U boat commander in First World War. Closely involved with the Confessing Church. Put into concentration camp in early days of Nazi regime and remained in camps until liberation in 1945.

General Friedrich Olbricht, senior Army officer in the resistance. Executed at army headquarters on Bendlerstrasse on night of 20 July 1944.

Colonel Albrecht Ritter Mertz von Quirnheim, succeeded Claus Stauffenberg as Chief of Staff to General Olbricht. Shot at army headquarters at Bendlerstrasse at midnight on 20 July 1944.

Major-General Hans Oster, deputy to Admiral Canaris. Played leading role in plans for September 1938 coup. Designated to become president of Reich military court if 1944 coup had succeeded. Arrested on 21 July 1944, held in concentration camps and executed at Flossenburg on 9 April 1945.

Field Marshal Erwin Rommel, Germany's most popular commander. Commander of Africa Corps 1941–1943, commander-in-chief in Italy and France 1944. Became potential Head of State after suicide of General Beck. Given choice by Hitler of committing suicide or facing trial for treason, he chose suicide on 14 October 1944.

Friedrich Dietlof Graf von der Schulenberg, Deputy Police President of Berlin, also involved with Kreisau Circle. Expelled from Nazi Party in 1940. Closely connected with Stauffenberg, Goerdler and von Moltke in resistance. Arrested after 20 July attempted coup. Executed 10 August 1944.

Lieutenant Fabian von Schlabrendorff, adjutant to Henning von Tresckow. Arrested after 20 July attempt. He came up before the People's Court on 3 February 1945 and survived the heavy air raid which killed Judge Freisler. His trial was re-scheduled for 16 March before the presiding judge, Dr Krohne, Vice-President of the People's Court. Schlabrendorff told the court that he had been tortured and that Frederick the Great had abolished torture in Prussia two hundred years earlier. His plea was accepted, the Chief Prosecutor dropped the indictment and the People's Court acquitted him and cancelled the arrest warrant. He was held in concentration camps and narrowly missed execution, but survived. From 1967 to 1975 he was a judge of the Constitutional Court of the Federal Republic of Germany.

Colonel Claus Schenk Graf von Stauffenberg, seriously wounded on 7 April 1943 in Western Desert. Designated to be Secretary of State in War Ministry after 20 July coup. Placed bomb in Hitler's conference room on 20 July 1944 and flew back from Rastenberg to Berlin. Executed at midnight at army headquarters on the Bendlerstrasse.

General Karl-Heinrich von Stulpnagel, Military Governor of France 1942–1944. A friend of General Beck since 1930. Involved in plans for September 1938 coup. When 1944 coup failed, he unsuccessfully attempted suicide. Executed 30 August 1944.

Major-General Henning von Tresckow, from 1942 onwards he planned several attacks on Hitler. Leader of the resistance on the Eastern Front. Committed suicide on 21 July 1944.

Ernst Freiherr von Weizsacker, State Secretary at the Foreign Office. Involved in the resistance. Survived the war.

Field Marshal Erwin von Witzleben, commander of Berlin military district in 1934 and took part in plans for coup in September 1938. Retired 1942 for health reasons. Agreed to assume command of Wehrmacht after 1944 coup. Arrested on 21 July. Executed on 8 August.

Peter Graf Yorck von Wartenberg, central figure in the Kreisau Circle with von Moltke and most of its meetings took place in his house on Hortensienstrasse. After much hesitation, agreed to idea of assassinating Hitler. Cousin of Stauffenberg. Executed 8 August 1944.

Notes

1. Clarita von Trott zu Solz, an account of Adam von Trott zu Solz, for his friends (later referred to as CvT, Memoir).
2. Giles MacDonogh, *A Good German*, p. 19. Quotation from Henry Malone, 'Adam von Trott zu Solz', unpublished Ph.D. thesis, University of Texas at Austin, 1980.
3. W.A. Visser't Hooft, *Memoirs*, p. 155.
4. John Marsh in a letter to Geoffrey Beck, 13 December 1989.
5. Conversations and correspondence with Clarita von Trott.
6. Albrecht von Kessel to Clarita von Trott.
7. Diana Hopkinson, *The Incense Tree*, p. 168.
8. C.E. Collins, Notes on Adam von Trott written for Adam's children, November 1946.
9. Collins, Notes, 1946.
10. Isaiah Berlin, Balliol Record 1986.
11. Professor Brock to Clarita von Trott, 1948.
12. Hopkinson, p. 111.
13. MacDonogh, p. 50.
14. *Manchester Guardian*, 5 March 1934.
15. Klemens von Klemperer, *A Noble Combat*, p. 327.
16. Hopkinson, p. 163.
17. Documents on British Foreign Policy 1919–1939, report from British Embassy in Berlin.
18. Ulrich von Hassell, *The Von Hassell Diaries*, p. 20.
19. Klemperer, p. 342.
20. Christabel Bielenberg, *The Past is Myself*, p. 49.
21. Allen Dulles, *Germany's Underground*, p. 48.
22. C.M. Bowra, *Memories, 1898–1939* (Cambridge, Mass., 1967).
23. Klemperer, p. 357.
24. Hopkinson, p. 165.
25. Hopkinson, p. 167.
26. Hopkinson, p. 168.
27. Richard Cockett, *David Astor and the Observer*, p. 59.
28. Bielenberg, p. 13.
29. Cockett, p. 62.
30. Cockett, p. 62.
31. Cockett, p. 62.
32. Visser't Hooft, p. 156.

Notes

33. Richard Lamb, *The Ghosts of Peace 1935–1945*, p. 256.
34. Lamb, p. 257.
35. Lamb, p. 257.
36. Lamb, p. 280.
37. Visser't Hooft, p. 158.
38. Count Helmuth James von Moltke, *A German of the Resistance, The Last Letters*.
39. von Moltke, *Letters to Freya, 1939–1945*, p. 411.
40. Christopher Sykes, *Troubled Loyalty*, p. 403.
41. Winston S. Churchill, *The Second World War*, volume 4, pp. 614–15.
42. Lamb, p. 220.
43. Ewan Butler, *Amateur Agent*.
44. Butler, quoting memorandum sent to London by Sir Victor Mallett, British envoy in Sweden.
45. Bielenberg, p. 143.
46. Marie (Missie) Vassiltchikov, *The Berlin Diaries*, p. 138.
47. F.O. file 371/39087.
48. Elizabeth Wiskemann, *The Europe I Saw*, London, 1968.
49. Vassiltchikov, p. 167.
50. C.v.T., Memoir.
51. Tatiana Metternich, *Five Passports in a Shifting Europe*, p. 193.
52. Fabian von Schlabrendorff, *The Secret War against Hitler*, p. 277; Peter Hoffman, *The History of the German Resistance, 1933–1945*, p. 375.
53. C.v.T., Memoir.
54. Letter to Clarita von Trott, 18 June 1944. C.v.T., Memoir.
55. The F.O. file on Adam's visit to Sweden was originally closed to the year 2000 because McEwan was a Secret Service agent. The file remains officially 'closed'.
56. MacDonogh, p. 281.
57. Vassiltchikov, p. 182.
58. MacDonogh, p. 292.
59. Vassiltchikov, p. 185.
60. Vassiltchikov, p. 186.
61. C.v.T., Memoir.
62. C.v.T., Memoir.
63. William Melchers' testimony (Bericht) in possession of Clarita von Trott.
64. Anton Gill, *An Honourable Defeat*, p. 254; von Schlabrendorff, pp. 294–5.
65. Vassiltchikov, p. 196.
66. Roger Manvell and Heinrich Fraenkel, *The July Plot*, p. 256, quoted from Otto John's account of July 20–24th.
67. C.v.T., Memoir.
68. Vassiltchikov, p. 201.
69. Vassiltchikov, p. 205.
70. Vassiltchikov, p. 211.

NOTES

71. Vassiltchikov, p. 225.
72. C.v.T., Memoir.
73. C.v.T., Memoir.
74. C.v.T., Memoir.
75. Lamb, p. 295.
76. Hansard, 2 August 1944.
77. Hansard, 27 January 1942; and Churchill, vol. 4, p. 59.
78. These words are widely quoted by Schlabrendorff and other German writers.
79. Schlabrendorff, p. 98.
80. Earl of Avon, *The Eden Memoirs*, vol. 2, p. 464.
81. F.O. 371/39062.
82. F.O. 371/39062.
83. Metternich, p. 104.
84. Tennyson, 'Ulysses'.

Bibliography

Avon, Earl of, *The Memoirs of Anthony Eden*, London, 1965.
Baigent, Michael and Leigh, Richard, *Secret Germany*, London, 1994.
Bielenberg, Christabel, *The Past is Myself*, London, 1968.
Bielenberg, Christabel, *Nazi Germany*, London, 1994.
Brysac, Shareen, *Resisting Hitler*, Oxford University Press, 2000.
Bullock, Alan, *Hitler: A Study in Tyranny*, 1962.
Butler, Ewan, *Amateur Agent*, London, 1963.
Churchill, Winston S., *The Second World War*:
    Vol. 1   The Gathering Storm, London, 1948.
    Vol. 2   Their Finest Hour, London, 1949.
    Vol. 3   The Grand Alliance, London, 1950.
    Vol. 4   The Hinge of Fate, London, 1951.
    Vol. 5   Closing the Ring, London, 1952.
    Vol. 6   Triumph and Tragedy, London, 1954.
Cockett, Richard, *David Astor and the Observer*, London, 1991.
Duff, Sheila Grant, *The Parting of Ways*, London, 1982.
Dulles, Allen Welsh, *Germany's Underground*, New York, 1947.
Fest, Joachim, *Hitler*, London, 1974.
Fest, Joachim, *Plotting Hitler's Death*, London, 1996.
Gilbert, Martin, *A History of the 20th Century*, vol. 2, London, 1998.
Gill, Anton, *An Honourable Defeat*, London, 1994.
Von Hassell, Ulrich, *The Von Hassell Diaries, 1938–1944*, London, 1948.
Hoffmann, Peter, *The History of the German Resistance, 1933–1945*, McGill-Queen's University Press, 1996.
Hopkinson, Diana, *The Incense Tree*, London, 1968.
John, Otto, *Twice Through the Lines*, London, 1972.
Kershaw, Ian, *Hitler*: vol 1, London 1998; vol. 2, London, 2000.
Von Klemperer, Klemens, *A Noble Combat*, OUP, 1998.
Von Klemperer, Klemens, *German Resistance against Hitler*, OUP, 1992.
Lamb, Richard, *The Ghosts of Peace*, 1935–1945, London, 1987.
Lamb, Richard, *The Drift to War*, London, 1989.
Leber, Annedore, *Conscience in Revolt*, London, 1957.
Leibholz-Bonhoeffer, *The Bonhoeffers: Portrait of a Family*, New York, 1971.
MacDonogh, Giles, *A Good German: Adam von Trott zu Solz*, London, 1989.
Manvell, Roger and Fraenkel, Heinrich, *The July Plot*, London, 1964.
Meehan, Patricia, *The Unnecessary War*, London, 1992.

Bibliography

Metternich, Tatiana, *Tatiana: Five Passports in a Shifting Europe*, London, 1976.
Micklem, Nathaniel, *The Box and the Puppets*, London, 1957.
Von Moltke, Count Helmuth James, *A German of the Resistance: The Last Letters*, OUP, 1947.
Von Moltke, Count Helmuth James *Letters to Freya 1939–1945,* London, 1991.
Robertson, Edwin, *The Shame and the Sacrifice: The Life and Martyrdom of Dietrich Bonhoeffer*, London, 1987.
Rose, Norman, *The Cliveden Set*, London, 2000.
Rothfels, Hans, *The German Opposition to Hitler*, London, 1961.
Von Schlabrendorff, Fabian, *Revolt against Hitler*, London, 1948; revised edition, *The Secret War Against Hitler*, Oxford, 1994.
Shirer, William L., *The Rise and Fall of the Third Reich*, New York, 1960.
Slack, Kenneth, *George Bell*, London, 1971.
Snyder, Louis L., *Encyclopedia of the Third Reich*, London, 1976.
Speer, Albert, *Spandau: The Secret Diaries*, London, 1976.
Stahlberg, Alexander, *Bounden Duty*, London, 1990.
Sykes, Christopher, *Troubled Loyalty: Adam von Trott zu Solz*, London, 1968.
Trevor-Roper, Hugh, *The Last Days of Hitler*, London, 1947.
Vassiltchikov, Marie, *The Berlin Diaries*, 1940–1945, London, 1985.
Visser't Hooft, W.A., *Memoirs*, London, 1973.
Watt, Donald Cameron, *How War Came*, London, 2001
Wiskemann, Elizabeth, *The Europe I Saw*, London, 1968.

The Times, March 1944 and July–September 1944.
The Daily Telegraph, July–September 1944.
Manchester Guardian, January–March 1934.
Hansard Parliamentary Reports.

Index

Abernathy, Robert, 5
Abwehr, 44, 46, 51, 70
Adams, Prof. W. G., 5
Africa, 44–5
Allies
  advances in Europe, 59
  bombing raids, 47
  lack of encouragement for conspirators, 49, 52, 57, 86
  landing in Normandy, 55
  making progress in war from 1943, 44–5
  need for armistice terms to be broadcast, 47–8
  policy of unconditional surrender, 47, 49
  reaction to failed coup, 78–82
  refusal to distinguish between 'good' and 'bad' Germans, 62, 80, 85
Almstrom, Frau, 47–8
America, 21, 22, 32
  see also Allies
Ash, Prof. Timothy Garton, x
Astor, David, 16, 27, 29
  with Adam, Plate 12
  letter to Adam 1939, 32
attempted coup (20 July 1944)
  attitude of British Government, 37–8, 49, 57, 70, 80–1
  consequences of failure, 84
  conspirators 'stepping into Nazis' shoes', 37
  day of attempt (20 July 1944), 40, 64–7
    conference room at Wolfsschanze, Plate 5
  execution of conspirators, 67
  German attitudes to conspirators, xii, xiii
  interrogations, 71–2
  military situation, 83–4
  names of chief conspirators, 37–8
  reaction of Allies, 78–82
  as 'symbolic act', xii
Attlee, Clement, 57

Ballestrem, Countess, 40
Balliol College, Oxford, 15–18
  correspondence with Diana Hubback, 16–17
  correspondence with Sheila Grant Duff, 16
  friendships, 15–17
  letter to parents, 15
Bargatzky, Walter, 83
Barrett, Louisa (Adam's nurse), 1–2
Beck, General Ludwig, Plate 3, 25, 26, 37, 51, 62, 67, 87
Bell, George, Bishop of Chichester, Plate 26, 37–8, 44, 87
Berg, Count, 68
Berlin
  Adam at school, 2
  Adam's room in the Pariserstrasse, 13
  execution at Plotzensee Prison, 76
  University, 13
Berlin, Isaiah, 16, 18
Bernstorff, Albrecht von, 40
Best, Captain Payne, 43–4
Bielenberg, Christabel, 25, 31
  conversation with Adam in Berlin 1944, 48–50
  memory of outbreak of war, 31–2

Index

Bielenberg, Peter, 25, 29, 31, 50, 62, 72
   with Adam von Trott and Johannes Winkelmann 1939, Plate 16
   arrest, 72–3
Blankenhorn, Herbert, 50–1
Bley, Curt, 71
Blum, Madonna, 62
Bodelschwingh, Heinz von, 56
Boeselager, Georg von, 60
Boeselager, Philipp Frieherr von, 60
Bonhoeffer, Dietrich, Plate 34, 37, 38, 87
   execution, 44
Bowra, Maurice, 27–8, 32
Brandt, Colonel, 65
Brandt, Willy, 56
Brock, Professor, 18
Bruning, Chancellor of Germany, 13
Butler, Ewan, 47

Cadogan, Sir Alexander, 52, 78
Canada, 21
Canaris, Admiral Wilhelm, 44, 51, 55, 87
Chamberlain, Neville, 25, 26
   announces war with Germany, 31
   meeting with Adam, 27
China, 21
Churchill, Winston, 24, 35, 43, 44, 56
   reaction to failed coup, 78–9
Clements, Dr Keith, x
Collins, Charles, 17
   with Adam at Imshausen, Plate 41
   postcard from Adam, Plate 39
Cox, Christopher, 18
Cripps, Sir Stafford, 21, 29, 34, 35, 36, 57, 76–7, 87
Crossman, Richard, 21
   comment on Adam's memorandum 1942, 35–37
Curtis, Lionel, 40, 41

Dassel, Hanover, 4
de Candole, Mrs Beatrix (Aunt Beatrix), 7, 9–10, 11–12
Dohnanyi, Hans von, 44
Douglas-Home, Sir Alec, 27
Duff, Sheila Grant, 16, 22, 24, 28
Dulles, Allen, 42, 44, 51, 55, 56
Dunglass, Lord (Sir Alec Douglas-Home), 27

Eden, Anthony, 24, 36, 38, 44, 79, 80
Eisenhower, General, 24, 45, 59, 84
Elliot, Robert, 44
English education, impressions of, 9, 12
European Union, xiii, 34

Falkenhausen, General Alexander von, 44, 51, 58, 87–8
Fellgiebel, General Fritz Erich, 64, 66, 88
Fest, Joachim, xii
Fisher, H. A. L. 21
France: Allied advances, 59
Frankfurter, Felix, 21, 28, 32
Franks, R. L., 11
Freisler, Judge Roland, 73, 88
Fromm, General Friedrich, 58, 61, 66, 67, 88
   with Stauffenberg, Keitel and Hitler, Plate 4
Furtwängler, Franz-Josef, 68

Geneva, 4, 5, 34, 44
Germany
   1930 elections, 13–14
   Adam's love of, 61, 62, 74
   after World War I, 2–3
   Allied bombing raids, 47
   Allied 'intention to destroy' (Goebbels), 44
   anti-semitism and pogroms, 19, 23–4
   'good' and 'bad' Germans, 62, 80, 81, 85
   low morale of army, 59
   military situation in July 1944, 83–4
   modern democratic values, xiii
   outbreak of war, 31
   possibility of 'deal' with England, 70
   rise of Nazis, 13–14
   see also Hitler, Adolf
Gersdorff, Maria, 69
Gestapo, 28, 47, 62, 71, 72, 80
Gisevius, Hans-Bernd, 55
Goebbels, 44, 47, 66, 75
Goerdler, Dr Carl Frierich, Plate 33, 38, 51, 56, 88
Göttingen University, 4–6, 13, Plate 28
Götz, Waltraud von, 68
Greene, Carlton, 81

INDEX

Haeften, Lieutenant Hans-Bernd von, 65, 66, 69, 73, 74, 88
   trial, Plate 18
Haeften, Lieutenant Werner von, 64, 67, 88
Hagen, Hans, 66
Halder, General Franz, 25–6, Plate 31, 51, 88
Halifax, Lord, 27, 43
Hammerstein, Lieutenant Ludwig Freiherr von, 37, 88
Hannoversch-Munden, Adam's school at, 2
Hansen, Colonel Georg, 55, 61–2
Harnack, Adolf von, 6
Harrison, Geoffrey, 36–7, 52
Harvey, Oliver, 81
Hase, General Paul von, 66, 88
Hassell, Ulrich von, 24, Plate 38, 44, 72, 88–9
Helldorf, Count Wolf Heinrich von, 73, 89
Hesse, 1, 19
Heusinger, General Adolf, 51, 64
Hewel, Walter, 27
Hill, Christopher, 27
Himmler, 73–4
Hindenburg, President, 17
Hinks, Roger, 42, 47, 56
Hitler, Adolf
   success in 1930 election, 13–14
   appointed Chancellor, 17
   plot led by Halder 1938, 25–6
   Munich agreement, 26, 27
   need for his overthrow, 34–5, 38, 48–9, 59, 60
   rumours of plots against 1944, 54–5
   military commanders turning against, 59–60
   urged to bring war to an end, 59–60
   abortive assassination attempt (11 July 1944), 60
   attempted coup (20 July 1944), 40, 64–7
   popularity in Germany, xii–xiii
   with Stauffenberg, Keitel and Fromm, Plate 4
   see also Germany
Hoepner, General Erich, 67, 89
Hofacker, Casar von, 61, 83

Hoffman, Conrad, 5
Hooft, William Adolf Visser't, 5, 34–5, 36, 89
Howard, Leslie, 24
Hubback, Diana, 16, 18, 23, 28–9

'Impressions of a German student in England', 12
Imshausen, 2, 5, 10, 12, Plate 17, Plate 40, Plate 41, 54, 74
Institute of Pacific Relations, Plate 13, 32
Ironside, Sir Edmund, 29
Israel, Wilfrid, 23–4, Plate 25, 89
Istanbul, 42, 46, 47
Italy: surrender, 43, 44

Jay, John, 1, 49
John, Otto, 70, 72, 89
   with brother Hans, Plate 36

Kaiser, 38
Kaiser Wilhelm Society for the Advancement of Science, 6
Keitel, Field Marshal Wilhelm, 64, 66, 89
   with Stauffenberg, Fromm and Hitler, Plate 4
Kempe, Inga, 56, 57
Kessel, Albrecht von, 13, 53
Kiep, Otto, 40, 46
Klausing, Captain Friedrich Karl, 60
Kleist, General Ewald von, 28
Kluge, Field Marshal Gunther von, 38, 60, 83–4, 89
Knapp–Fisher, James, 57
Koelle, William, 14
Kostring, Major-General Ernst, 58
Kreisau Circle, xiii, 39–41, 58, 77
Kuhn, Major, 69
Kunzer, 40

Langbehn, Carl, 44
Leipholdt, with Adam, Trump, Hans Felix Richter and Alexander Worth, Plate 27
letters to parents, 7–8, 9, 10, 11
Leuschner,, 38, 51
Leverkuhn, Paul, 46
Lindsay, A. D., 16, 21, 33
Lothian, Lord, 27, 70
Louis Ferdinand, Prince, 38

Index

Loxley, P. H., 52

MacEwan, David, 56
Mahnke, Dr Horst, 73
Mallett, Sir Victor, 38
Manchester Guardian, 19
Mansfield College, Oxford, ix, x, xi, 7–12
   Adam von Trott Memorial Lectures, x
   finances and accommodation, 7–8
   German Club, 10
   summary of studies, 11
Manstein, Field Marshal Erich von, 89
Marsh, John, 8
Marshall, Thomas, 35, 80–1
Marxism, 13
Melchers, Wilhelm, 65, 68
Metternich, Paul, 54–5
Moltke, Count Helmuth James von, 21, 28, 39, 44, 89–90
   arrest and execution, 40–1
   on trial 1945, Plate 2
Montgomery, Field Marshal Sir Bernard, 60, 78
Montgomery, Hugh, 13
Muller, Josef, 44
Munchhausen, Ernst Friedemann Freiherr von, 4
Munich agreement, 26, 27
Munich University, 4, 56

Nazism
   Adam's attitude to, 10, 17, 19–20
   and anti-Jewish pogrom, 24
   German military distrust of Nazi Party, 59
   Nazi–Soviet Pact, 29
   and non-Nazis, 26, 85
   rise of, 13–14, 21
   see also Germany; Hitler, Adolf
Neurath, 80
Nicholson, Brigadier Claude, xii
Niemöller, Martin, 63, 90

Olbricht, General Friedrich, 51, 58, 61, 67, 90
Oster, Major-General Hans, 25, 44, 51, 90
Oxford, Plate 10, 48, 86
   Adam's impression of, 9, 18

Balliol College, 15–18
Mansfield College, x, xi, 7–12

Patton, General, 84
plots against Hitler *see* attempted coup (20 July 1944); Hitler, Adolf
Poelchau, Dr Harold, 77
Popitz, Johannes, 44
Potsdam, 1

Quirnheim, Albrecht Ritter Mertz von, 61, 67, 90

Ranzau, Josias von, with Adam, Hans Felix Richter and Alexander Worth, Plate 24
Rastenburg, 64
Read, Miss, 9
Remer, Major Ernst, 66–7
Rhodes Scholarship, 14–18
Richter, Hans Felix, with Adam, Alexander Worth and Josias von Rantzau, Plate 24
Richter, Hans Felix, with Adam, Trump, Alexander Worth and Leipholdt, Plate 27
'rightness' of conspiracy to kill, 8
Roberts, Frank, 52
Rommel, Field Marshal Erwin, 52, 59–60, 62, 79, 83, 90
Roosevelt, President, 28, 32, 42–3, 84
Rowse, A. L., 14
Rundstedt, Field Marshal Gerd von, 51, 59

Sandys, Diana, 28
Sandys, Duncan, 28
Saurma von der Jeltsch, Baron Anton (Tony Saurma), 73
Schacht, 38, 80
Scherpenberg, Hilger von, 40
Schlabrendorf, Lieutenant Fabian von, 28, 55, 68, 79, 90–1
Schmidz, Dr, 73
Schoenfeld, Hans, 37
Scholten, G. J., 5, 12
Schonburg, Loremarie, 69, 72
Schulenburg, Count Werner von der, 58, 75

Index

Schulenburg, Friedrich Dietlof Graf von der, 61, 90
Schumacher, Fritz, 14
Schwanenfeld, Schwerin von, 62
Schweinitz, Ebehard von (Adam's uncle), 13, 14, 25
Schweinitz, Lothar von (Adam's grandfather), 1
Selbie, Revd Dr William Boothby, 5–6, 7–8, 9, 12, 14, 15–16, Plate 32
  letter to *Manchester Guardian*, 19
Selbie, R. J., 5
Six, Dr, 69, 70, 73, 74
socialism, 13
Solf Circle, 40, 44
Stalin, 43, 49
Stauffenberg, Berthold, 61, 63
Stauffenberg, Colonel Claus Schenk Graf von, 53, 55, 57–8, 61–2, 63, 71, 72, 91, Plate 29
  attempted coup (20 July 1944), 64–5, 66, 67
  with Fromm, Keitel and Hitler, Plate 4
Stieff, Major-General Helmuth, 60
Stockholm
  British Legation, 47–8
Strong, Tracy, 5
Student Christian Movement (SCM), 5, 11, 44
Stulpnagel, General Karl-Heinrich von, 26, 44, 83, 91
Stuttgart, 55

Daily Telegraph, 76
Thadden, Elizabeth von, 40
Tiefenbacher, Clarita *see* Trott zu Solz, Clarita von (née Tiefenbacher) (Adam's wife)
Times, 46, 76
Toynbee, Arnold, 35
Tresckhow, Major-General Henning von, Plate 30, 55, 60, 68–9, 91
Trott zu Solz, Adam von:
  Plates: about 1935, Plate 6, Plate 11
  in 1932, Plate 1
  with Alexander Worth, Hans Felix Richter and Josias von Rantzau, Plate 24
  with Hans Felix Richter, Trump, Alexander Worth and Leipholdt, Plate 27
  with Johannes Winkelmann and Peter Bielenberg 1939, Plate 16
  personal qualities and views:
  appearance and character, 4, 5, 8, 11, 15, 35, 42, 85
  facing death 'with resignation' (Clarita von Trott), 54
  friendships, 15–17
  need to oppose Hitler and Nazism, 17, 19–20, 24, 48–9, 50
  patriotism, 61, 62, 68, 74
  political views and Nazism, 10, 13–14, 17, 19–20, 35
  religion/moral values, 5, 8, 53, 54, 68–9
  vision for post-war Europe, 35, 39, 40
  correspondents
  Clarita, 54–5, 63, 74, 75–6
  David Astor, 32, 33
  Diana Hubback, 23, 29
  parents, 7–8, 9, 10, 11, 15, 18, 76
  Sheila Grant Duff, 22, 24, 25
  life before the war
  birth and family background, 1
  parents, Plate 7, Plate 9
  school in Berlin and Kassel, 2
  boarding school in Hannoversch-Munden, 2
  end of World War I, 2–3
  Universities of Munich and Göttingen, 4–6, Plate 28
  as a student, Plate 8
  Geneva and SCM 1928, 4–5
  SCM conference in Liverpool 1929, 5
  Mansfield College, Oxford, x, 7–12
  essay: 'Impressions of a German student in England', 12
  Berlin University, 13
  return to Göttingen 1930, 13
  German elections 1930, 13–14
  doctoral dissertation, 14
  Balliol College, Oxford as Rhodes Scholar, x, 14, 15–18
  Hitler appointed Chancellor, 17
  concern about fate of Germany, 17–18
  postcard: Christmas 1933, Plate 39
  return to Germany 1933, 18, 48

Index

legal training in Germany 1933–1936, 19–20
return to England 1935, 20
travels in Far East and North America, 21–2
death of father 1938, 23
return to Germany, 23
anti-Jewish pogroms, 23–4
decision to oppose Hitler, 24
hears of earlier plot against Hitler, 25
plan to oppose Hitler, 26–30
visit to Downing St, 27
last meeting with Sheila Grant Duff, 28
last meeting with Diana Hubback, 28–9
memorandum: 'Inner Political Situation in Germany Today', 29–30

wartime
outbreak of war, 31–2
in America 1939 and decision to return home, 32
marriage to Clarita, 33, Plate 35
wartime travels, 34
in Davos 1942, Plate 14
visit to Visser't Hooft in Geneva, 34
memorandum to Cripps for support and federal Europe, 34–5
responses to memorandum, 35–7
appeal to George Bell, Bishop of Chichester, 37–8
names of chief conspirators, 37–8
meetings of Kreisau Circle, 39
infiltration and arrests, 40
Operation Valkyrie, 42, 61, 66
efforts to raise interest in anti-Hitler plots, 42, 44
visit to Basle 1943, Plate 15
Vermehren's posting to Istanbul, 46–7
views given in Stockholm 1944, 47–8
meeting with Blankenhorn 1944, 50–1
meeting with Dulles in Switzerland, 51
Allied scepticism about conspiracy, 51–2

meeting with Elizabeth Wiskemann in Switzerland 1944, 52–3
return to Germany: offices bombed, 53
with von Kessel in Italy, 53–4
last meeting with family in Imshausen, 54
rumours of plot circulating, 54–5
Allied landings in Normandy, 55
last meeting with Clarita, 55
visit to Stockholm: memorandum to British Government, 56
eve of abortive assassination attempt, 61
taken ill in Stockholm 1944, 56–7
abortive assassination attempt (11 July 1944), 60–1
meetings before July 20th attempt, 61–3
attempted coup, July 20th, 64–6

after the failed coup
Adam refuses to escape, 68–70
talk with Missie Vassiltchikov, 69–70
arrest by Gestapo, 71
plans for his rescue, 72–3
trial and sentence, Plate 19, Plate 20, Plate 22, 73, 74
letters from prison, 74, 75, 76
execution, 76
memorial stone, Plate 21
memorial cross, Plate 23
Adam's verdict on failed coup, x, 68–9

Trott zu Solz, Clarita von (née Tiefenbacher) (Adam's wife), 12, 47, 54, 66
with Adam, Plate 35
arrest, 74
last time with Adam, 55
letters from Adam in prison, 74, 75–6
memory of Adam's last visit home, 54
Trott zu Solz, Eleonore von (née von Schweinitz) (Adam's mother), 1, Plate 7
church leaders' meeting at Dassel, 4–5
letter from Adam in prison, 76
Trott zu Solz, Heinrich von, 50
Trott zu Solz, Werner von (Adam's brother), 10

Index

Trump, with Adam, Hans Felix Richter, Alexander Worth and Leipholdt, Plate 27
'unconditional surrender' of Germany, xiv, 42–4, 47, 80, 81
Unruh, Adalbert von, 25

Vassiltchikov, Missie, x, 51
   with Adam, 61, 62–3, 69–70
   and Adam's arrest and imprisonment, 71, 72, 75
Vassiltchikov, Tatiana, 54
Vermehren, Erich, 46–7

Walter, Fraulein, 49
Weimar Republic, 13
Weizsacher, Ernst Freiherr von, 26, 27, 72, 80, 91
Werth, Alexander, 66, 72
Wheeler-Bennett, 80
Williams, Brigadier Edgar, 78

Wilson, Geoffrey, 10, 26
Winkelmann, Johannes with Adam and Peter Bielenberg 1939, Plate 16
Wiskemann, Elizabeth, 36–7
   memory of Adam in Switzerland 1944, 52–3
Witzleben, Field Marshal Erwin von, 25, 26, Plate 37, 38, 78, 91
Woodward, E. L., 21
World War I: aftermath, 2–3
Worth, Alexander, 56, 70
   with Adam, Hans Felix Richter and Josias von Rantzau, Plate 24
   with Adam, Leipholdt, Trump and Hans Felix Richter, Plate 27

Yorck von Wartenberg, Peter Graf, 39, 44, 57–8, 61, 91

Zeitzler, General Kurt, 51
Zimmern, Sir Alfred, 35

www.ingramcontent.com/pod-product-compliance
Lightning Source LLC
Chambersburg PA
CBHW070239240426
43673CB00044B/1853